JOINT PROPERTY

EVERYTHING YOU MUST KNOW
TO SAVE TIME, TROUBLE, AND MONEY
ON YOUR JOINTLY OWNED PROPERTY

by Alexander A. Bove, Jr.

A Fireside Book
Published by Simon and Schuster
New York

To
Cathy
Andrea
and
Alexander III

A Fireside Book
Published by Simon and Schuster
A Division of Gulf & Western Corporation
Simon & Schuster Building
Rockefeller Center
1230 Avenue of the Americas
New York, New York 10020
FIRESIDE and colophon are registered trademarks
of Simon & Schuster
Designed by
Irving Perkins Associates

Manufactured in the United States of America
Printed and bound by Fairfield Graphics
3   5   7   9   10   8   6   4   2

Library of Congress Cataloging in Publication Data

Bove, Alexander A., 1982.
    Joint property.
    (A Fireside Book)
    Includes index.
    1. Joint tenancy—United States. 2. Joint ownership of personal
property—United States. 3. Inheritance and succession—United States.
I. Title.
KF619.B68   346.7304'2   82-5497
                        347.30642   AACR2
ISBN 0-671-44967-2

CONTENTS

ACKNOWLEDGMENTS

I would like to express my sincere appreciation to my partners, Stanley Charmoy and Ron McDougald, for their support and patience, to Rollie Flynn for her perceptiveness and ability to recognize a promising project, and to my favorite secretary, Judy Santoro.

INTRODUCTION

THIS IS A BOOK ABOUT JOINT property—you know, ownership by two people so that either one can easily get it on death or other "emergency"? Or so we hope. Joint property is that popular but troublesome character constantly popping up in just about every family picture. That's right, *troublesome.*

Did you know that the surviving joint owner does not always get the property? Or that joint property can bypass your will and leave out children? Or can cost your estate thousands in needless extra taxes? Or does not necessarily avoid probate?

In this book I address every one of these points and, of course, many more. You'll find out how to identify the problems in your own situation and how to avoid them, how to tell when you have a *true* joint ownership, and when you don't—*and* what to do about it.

For instance, how can you be sure that the funds in your joint bank account will pass to the survivor? Many such accounts are not considered a "true" joint ownership and are easily attacked unless a specific intent for survivorship is shown. Chapter 7 explains the importance of establishing your intent and tells you exactly how to do it.

And do you know the difference between property held in the names of Jack *and* Jill versus Jack *or* Jill? As far as survivorship goes, there is no difference, but a check made out to Jack *or* Jill could be cashed by either, while one payable to Jack *and* Jill must be signed by both. In *either* case, however, Jack and Jill each have a right to use half the property or money. This will give you an idea of some of the traps of joint property.

The book is designed for use in every state, but not all state laws are the same. Although the basic principles discussed in the book apply nationally, you should check the laws in your state to determine the effect on your particular situation. For example, when you see that a "tenancy by the entirety" (a special form of joint ownership for husband and wife) might offer some protection from creditors, you may want to consider using this form of joint ownership. However, if you live in one of the twenty-six states (listed in Chapter 4) that does not recognize a tenancy by the entirety, or if you live in one of the eight community states (listed in Chapter 11), you may have to seek a different alternative.

Finally, the book has been written for your general reference and information, so that at any time you can refer directly to any chapter that interests you. If, for example, you have a question about joint bank accounts, Chapter 7 will tell you everything you want to know about the subject. If you're getting a divorce (or worried about one), you may start with Chapter 9 on Joint Tenancy and Divorce, then wend your way to the front of the book. In short, the book is designed to help you.

These vital but misunderstood areas of the law can be very important to you and to your family's welfare, and with a modest investment of time and attention you will be enlightened, guided, and perhaps even a little entertained.

Alex Bove

1

JOINT PROPERTY AND OTHER CONFUSING FORMS OF CO-OWNERSHIP

THE MURDER OF ENID PINNOCK

NO ONE KNEW JUST WHEN Granville Pinnock decided to strangle his wife, Enid, or whether this was part of a plan that ended by his hanging himself. Since neither Granville nor his wife is alive to tell us, we can only speculate.

Granville and Enid Pinnock were married in 1963. In 1973 they purchased a home at 4103 Lowerrie Place, in the Bronx, New York, taking title as "tenants by the entirety." As most married couples do, they also opened a joint savings account; theirs was with the Bronx office of the Chase Manhattan Bank. Granville took a job at the Glenwood Management Company as a welder and everything seemed to be going well—except their marriage.

Enid was a very domineering person and always chided Granville, often in public. She embarrassed and belittled him in front of friends, sometimes even made him cry, but he still loved her. When he learned she was seeking a divorce, Granville was crushed, and for the next two weeks he wasn't the same. Then one evening in January 1975 he arrived home after Enid was asleep. He stared at her for a while pondering their lives together and their bleak future, when he discovered a note that Enid had left. It was a suicide note saying she had taken poison. Granville was stricken at the thought of being left alone, without Enid. Taking no chances that the poison might not work, Granville found a length of rope, went to Enid's room, and strangled her in her sleep. He then wrote his own suicide note, went to the basement, and successfully hanged himself.

Granville and Enid had no children. Granville left his parents as his heirs, and Enid left a sister, Cyselin Stephenson, who stood to inherit her estate. The question was, however, how should the jointly held property be treated? Should it go to Granville's parents through his estate or through Enid's estate to Enid's sister Cyselin? As "everyone" knows, joint property should go to the survivor on the death of one of the joint tenants. Since Granville obviously survived his wife, his estate should be entitled to all the joint property.

There is, however, something clearly wrong with this reasoning, because Granville himself caused the death of Enid, the other joint tenant. Should one joint tenant who murders another joint tenant be allowed to receive the jointly held property? Doesn't joint property automatically pass to the survivor regardless of the circumstances of the death of a joint tenant? This is the understanding that most people have of joint property, but in the words of Composer George Gershwin, "it ain't necessarily so."

In the Pinnock case the court treated each item of property separately. The residence was held as a tenancy by the entirety. This is a special form of joint tenancy for husbands and wives, where neither, acting alone, can terminate the tenancy, and on the death of either, all would go to the survivor.

Because Granville's rights in the property were not completely his until Enid's death and because it was he who caused her death, the court reasoned that Granville had "forfeited whatever rights of survivorship he had when he became the survivor solely by dint of his wrongfully extinguishing the life of his wife." Therefore, it was held that the residence should pass to Enid's heirs, and nothing (of the real estate) to Granville's heirs.

That was how the residence was treated. The joint bank account lent itself to a slightly different approach. It is true, the court said, that the perpetrator of a crime should not be entitled to benefit from his wrongful act, and that this should apply as well to jointly held property. However, what rights did Granville Pinnock have in the joint bank account prior to Enid's death, and what rights would he gain on the death of his wife, had he not caused her death? First, each of the two joint tenants in the bank account was entitled to a present one-half interest in the proceeds of the account, and during their lives, each could withdraw up to one-half of the account without liability to the other joint tenant, according to the court's reasoning.

By his wrongful act, Granville forfeited his right to succeed to Enid's half of the account, but, the court said, he could not be deprived of his own one-half of the account because this is a right that he had independent of his wrongful act. He could have withdrawn up to one-half the account at any time simply by withdrawing the funds. Therefore, it was held that one-half the account belonged to Granville's estate and one-half to Enid's estate.

The different results in this case for the different types of property were not unusual. Disposition of joint property at death should never be taken for granted, and the cases involving murder of a joint tenant merely serve to illustrate more dramatically the complexities hidden under this simple facade.

The New York court that decided the Pinnock case attempted to make the most equitable decision possible under New York law. The same case, however, may well have been given different treatment in Missouri, Illinois, or California, where the laws and preceding cases are not quite the same. In fact, it is quite possible for the same general fact pattern to produce different results even in the same state.

JOINT OWNERSHIP—
AS DECEIVING AS IT IS SIMPLE

ALTHOUGH THE MURDER OF one joint tenant by another may be somewhat unusual, no individual joint tenant is immortal and death of a joint tenant must be considered when placing property in joint names. The Pinnock case is merely an illustration of how joint ownership may not necessarily produce the results anticipated by the joint owners. Facts, circumstances, and the law can all be co-authors of the will of a joint tenant.

It takes little imagination to observe that Granville Pinnock was totally unconcerned with the disposition of his property when he murdered his wife or when he hanged himself. On the other hand, perhaps he felt that because it was jointly owned, the property would be disposed of automatically and without trouble.

In fact, this is the attitude generally held by most families with joint property. Joint ownership is probably the most popular form of family ownership of property, while at the same time the least understood. This lack of understanding and resulting misuse make it as prevalent *in* the courts as it is outside. It is the subject of as much if not more litigation than any other single probate (death-oriented) issue. When viewed in the light of an entire estate, "simple" joint property can produce surprising and costly tax and legal complications. It can generate a tax liability that could otherwise have been avoided. It can create family dissension by superseding a will that contains provisions that conflict with the transfer to the surviving joint tenant. While appearing to provide for a spouse, it can actually operate to exclude children. And, somewhat like marriage, it is often much more difficult to undo than it is to do.

It is estimated that more than three-fourths of all the real estate owned by husbands and wives in the United States is held in joint tenancy. And joint ownership of property by families is certainly not limited to real estate. If we add joint bank accounts, joint ownership of stocks and bonds, and joint safe deposit boxes, we can easily see that this form of ownership is far and away the "people's choice."

What is the reason for this overwhelming popularity of joint ownership? Perhaps the answer is popularity itself. Just about everyone is aware of it and we all think we understand it. Placing property in joint names almost comes naturally. It is so easy, and it offers the protection and peace of mind that the survivor will receive the property if one joint owner dies—or does it? There are hundreds, perhaps thousands of court decisions that don't necessarily uphold this principle. This book will not only point out these pitfalls and problems but will also offer some solutions, ways of avoiding the problems, and some alternatives to joint ownership. Because the concepts of joint ownership can be complicated and elusive, it may be helpful to begin by explaining the nature and the different types of joint forms of ownership and how they are treated.

DIFFERENT TYPES OF CO-TENANCIES AND THEIR CHARACTERISTICS

QUESTION	JOINT PROPERTY	TENANCY BY THE ENTIRETY	TENANCY IN COMMON
Survivorship rights?	Yes	Yes	No
Right to sell share?	Yes	No	Yes
Right to divide?	Yes	No	Yes
Can creditors reach share?	Yes	Maybe	Yes
Included in estate?	Yes (unless w/spouse then one-half)	Yes (one-half)	Only your share

JOINT PROPERTY V. TRUST

	JOINT PROPERTY	TRUST
Avoids probate?	Probably	Yes
Can save estate taxes?	No	Yes
Helps avoid creditor's attack?	No	Yes
Provides for the unexpected?	No	Yes
Affected by disability of owner?	Yes	No
Affected by simultaneous death?	Yes	No
Affected by divorce?	Yes	No
Easy to obstruct?	Yes	No
Can provide for spouse, children, and grandchildren?	No	Yes
Can protect from creditors of beneficiaries?	No	Yes
Can predict outcome?	No	Yes
Reduces overall costs and expenses?	No	Yes

2

THE BASICS
OF JOINT
TENANCY

WHEN MORE THAN ONE PERSON own the *same piece* of property at the *same time,* they are said to be "co-tenants" of that property. Joint tenancy is just one of the forms of co-tenancy; the other popular forms of co-tenancy include tenancy by the entirety, tenancy in common, and tenancy by partnership. (Community property could also be considered a form of co-tenancy. This is dealt with separately in Chapter 11.) The word "tenant" as used in "joint tenant" or in one of the other forms of co-tenancy should not be confused with its more popular use, in which, for example, a person who rents a room or apartment is considered a tenant and the owner of the property is the landlord. Although in both uses the tenant has the right of possession of the property, the landlord/tenant relationship is quite different from the relationship of co-tenants to each other. Our use of the word tenant in this book will always be in the context of the co-tenancy or common ownership of property. In all co-tenancies the underlying characteristic and essential element is that each co-tenant is entitled to possession and enjoyment of the *whole* property, at least during the period of co-tenancy.

This right of possession and enjoyment is referred to as an "undivided" interest, since the property actually remains undivided. If it were divided, each party would own his or her separate share and there would no longer be a co-tenancy. For example, if Peter and Paul jointly purchase a truckload of lumber, they are co-tenants in the undivided load of lumber on the truck. However, the property is easily divisible, and once they divide the load into each respective share, their interests are separated and neither has a right to possess the other's share. The co-tenancy is terminated.

On the other hand, if two people own an automobile jointly, each joint tenant has the right to use it at any given time, and neither can lawfully exclude the other from using it. However, because of the nature of some property (such as an automobile), it cannot be divided or it would be highly impractical to do so, and both cannot use it simultaneously. Therefore (as with all co-tenancies) the co-tenants must have an agreeable arrangement for its use. (The responsibilities tenants have to each other are discussed in Chapter 5.)

YOU DON'T "INHERIT" JOINT PROPERTY

ANOTHER POINT CRITICAL TO your understanding of joint property is the way it operates to "pass" property from one joint owner to another. That is, one does *not* "inherit" joint property! The property is actually transferred *at the time the joint ownership is created*. On the subsequent death of a joint owner there is no further need for a legal transfer or inheritance to the surviving joint owner. At the moment of death of a joint tenant, the deceased joint tenant's share "disappears" and the surviving joint tenant (or tenants if there are more than one) becomes the sole owner of the property.

WHO MAY BE JOINT TENANTS?

OF COURSE, ANY TWO (OR more) persons can be joint tenants. There are no age requirements, except that in some cases, such as with real estate or securities, having a *minor* as a joint tenant can interfere with a subsequent transfer or sale of the jointly held property. In general, it is *not* a good idea to have a minor as a joint tenant.

Ownership of property in joint tenancy, by the very nature of its most distinctive characteristic—the right of survivorship— suggests that it is reserved to natural persons. That is, a corporation or a partnership or a trust may not act as a "true" joint tenant.

There may be, however, a legal situation created by contract or other agreement whereby, for example, a corporation and an individual enter into an arrangement with respect to certain property whereby on the death of the individual the corporation will own the entire property, and likewise, if the corporation is dissolved or liquidated (a legal "death"), the individual would own the property. Although this could be technically construed as a joint tenancy, such arrangements are extremely involved and intricate from a legal and tax standpoint and should be avoided if possible.

In general, the co-tenancies contemplated in this book deal with natural (adult) persons. If a joint tenant turns out to be a minor and the joint tenancy involves real estate or securities, a guardian or custodian may have to be appointed for the minor, and the guardian or custodian would then act as joint tenant on behalf of the minor.

WHAT TYPE OF PROPERTY MAY BE HELD IN JOINT TENANCY?

UNDER EARLY COMMON LAW, only real estate could be held in a joint tenancy, but before long other types of property could also be jointly held, and it is now generally recognized that a joint tenancy may exist in just about every type of property interest, real, personal or otherwise, including securities, bank accounts, patents, copyrights, jewelry, automobiles, furniture and fixtures, insurance policies, safe deposit boxes, and even animals.

HOW A JOINT TENANCY DIFFERS FROM TENANCY IN COMMON

THE BASIC DIFFERENCE between a joint tenancy and a tenancy in common is the "right of survivorship." This means that when a joint tenant dies, the survivor (or survivors) takes the whole of the property, but with a tenancy in common, the survivor merely continues to hold the same interest he had before the death of his co-tenant. The interest or share in the name of the deceased co-tenant passes through his estate, by way of his will if he had one, or if not, according to the laws of the state of his permanent residence (domicile) at the time of his death. (See Chapter 3 for a complete explanation of the tenancy in common.)

COMPLICATIONS OF JOINT TENANCY

THE RIGHT OF SURVIVORSHIP unique to the joint tenancy has developed such an attraction that it is almost universally accepted as a practical way to hold savings, securities, real estate, etc. What is normally overlooked is that a survivorship interest can be hopelessly complicated and even obstructed by conflicting provisions in a will, or by embittered beneficiaries who believe that they were cheated out of their funds, or by the executor or administrator of an estate who carries out his duty to collect the assets of the estate in spite of objections by the surviving joint tenant.

Another trap that many joint owners inadvertently may face is the haphazard distribution of the jointly held property when the last joint owner dies. In other words, on Larry's death the property he held jointly with his wife, Louise, will automatically pass to her, but what then happens on Louise's death?

The prospect of the "automatic transfer" on survivorship frequently overshadows the fact that the jointly held property will ultimately end up passing through the survivor's probate estate. Many people mistakenly feel that with joint property there is no need for a will. *Few statements could be more costly and misleading!* At some point, all but the last joint owner will die, and the property which was at one time jointly held will be owned solely by the survivor (unless he or she creates a new joint tenancy), and will pass through the survivor's estate. For example, if Joe and Catherine have a joint bank account, on Joe's death it will belong solely to Catherine. If she then dies, the account must pass through her probate estate. This commonly overlooked trap must be considered carefully, for the property could end up far afield of the original joint owners' intentions. And then, of course, there is the possibility of a simultaneous death of the joint owners. What then?

SIMULTANEOUS DEATH OF JOINT OWNERS

ALL THE STATES HAVE adopted what is referred to as the Uniform Simultaneous Death Act. This law provides for prescribed orders of death for purposes of inheritance when two or more people die simultaneously. For example, A's will states "I leave all my property to B" but A and B die at the same time. Does B still inherit A's property? The same problem can apply to joint tenants. If husband and wife own property jointly, they may feel sure that the property will go to the survivor so there is no need for a will. But if they die at the same time, who is the survivor? The Uniform Simultaneous Death Act has the answer—*both* are considered survivors!

In other words, under the Act, unless otherwise provided for by will or "other instrument," each joint tenant is considered to have survived the other in case of simultaneous death. The effect of this brain-teasing result on joint property of husband and wife is to divide the property equally, so that half passes through the wife's estate and half through the husband's estate. This could double the fees and administrative expenses and double the delays involved in settling the estates. It may also cost one or both estates substantial amounts in additional estate taxes which could have been avoided had the couple executed wills. The Uniform Simultaneous Death Act provides that in the case of a simultaneous death the deceased, in a will or trust, may declare who survives him. In the case of joint property, the designation of a survivor would cause the property to avoid the (probate) estate of one of the joint owners, as was their intent in the first place. Typical language might be "In the event my wife and I die simultaneously or under circumstances where it is impossible to tell which of us died first, then my wife shall be deemed to have survived me." If this language is used in a husband's will or trust, any reference to simultaneous death in his wife's will or trust must be consistent, otherwise the purpose will be defeated. That is, the language suggested above would warrant a statement in the wife's will that on a simultaneous death *she* will be considered the survivor.

TERMINATION OF A JOINT TENANCY

HAVING A JOINT TENANCY CAN at times be more involved than this "simple" form of ownership would lead us to assume, and even the possibility of complications is generally overlooked by the co-tenants. Similarly, when a joint tenancy is created, the joint tenants seldom give thought to its termination or how it may come about. Termination may be caused several ways—by an act of one of the joint tenants or by agreement of all the tenants, by a court of law or, of course, by death of all the co-tenants but one. In any case the net result is the same: once the joint tenancy is terminated, the distinctive right of survivorship is extinguished.

TERMINATION BY ACT OF A JOINT TENANT

ANY ACT OF A JOINT TENANT that transfers his share of the property will destroy the joint tenancy, at least as to that tenant's share. If there are two joint tenants and one sells his or her share to a stranger, the stranger does not become a joint tenant, but rather the joint tenancy is terminated and the stranger becomes a tenant in common (see Chapter 3) with the other original joint tenant. On the other hand, if there were three or more joint tenants and one of them transfers his interest to a stranger, the stranger still becomes a tenant in common with the other joint tenants while they remain joint tenants as to each other. For example, if A, B, and C are joint tenants with rights of survivorship and A sells his undivided one-third interest to a stranger, then the stranger would be a tenant in common with B and C, but B and C would still be joint tenants as to each other. Therefore, on the death of B, C would own two-thirds of the property and vice versa. But on the death of the stranger, his share would pass through his (the stranger's) estate. If the stranger sold the interest back to the tenant from whom he purchased it, this would not revive the joint tenancy since the essential legal elements have been destroyed.

Of course, if all the joint tenants sell or transfer the jointly held property, the joint tenancy is destroyed since the property is gone. However, if the property was sold, it is generally held that the proceeds from the sale of joint property are likewise held in joint tenancy, until divided.

If the joint tenants agree, the joint tenancy may be terminated anytime they wish. Such an agreement, of course, should never be oral, since there is enough potential for confusion in the original situation.

TERMINATION BY COURT ORDER

IF THE PARTIES CANNOT AGREE and a termination of the joint tenancy is desired, either (or any) of the joint tenants may ask a court to "partition" the joint tenancy. A partition is a legal proceeding in which the court, after review of the request, may order the property divided into the respective shares of the joint owners. This terminates the joint tenancy and leaves each of the respective parties with a share of the property. They are *not* left as tenants in common, since the property is *actually divided* and the shares distributed. If the property is not divisible, as in the case of a building or a painting, the court will usually order a sale, then a division of the proceeds. (The right to partition is discussed in more detail in Chapter 5.)

Death of a joint tenant also terminates the joint tenancy if there are only two joint tenants. If there are three or more joint tenants, the joint tenancy will continue until the death of the last joint tenant, and will then pass to his or her estate.

SUMMARY

JOINT OWNERSHIP OF PROPERTY is unjustifiably popular when viewed in the light of the problems it can create. On the other hand, it can also provide certain conveniences and savings in administrative expenses and time in settling estates, if used and applied with care and with knowledge of its risks and shortcomings. Property placed in joint names with another should be supported by letters, agreements, statements, provisions in a will, trust, or other documents confirming the intent of the joint owners that the survivor should take the entire account, if that is the intent; otherwise, another form of ownership should be considered. Care should be exercised to avoid conflicting provisions in a will or other document leaving the joint property to someone else. Joint accounts should be used sparingly and with deliberation; they are not a substitute for a will. Finally, joint ownership provides no guarantee of immortality; therefore, each of the joint owners should have a will, and the wills should consider the possibility of a simultaneous death of the joint owners, as well as the disposition of the property on the death of the last surviving joint owner.

3

TENANCY IN COMMON

AN EXPLANATION OF "TENANCY in common" is essential to a discussion on joint tenancy, because even though it may sometimes be intentionally created, a tenancy in common is what usually results from the failure to create a valid joint tenancy. In other words, it (the tenancy in common) is often created by accident or mistake.

DIFFERENCES BETWEEN A TENANCY IN COMMON AND A JOINT TENANCY

THE BASIC DIFFERENCE between a tenancy in common and a joint tenancy is the *right of survivorship,* which exists in a valid joint tenancy but which *does not exist in a tenancy in common.*

Under the tenancy in common, the share of a deceased tenant passes through his "estate," that is, as he may direct by his will, or by some other legal arrangement. It will *not* automatically pass to the surviving co-tenant as it would if it were a valid joint tenancy.

For example, Bernard and his brother Bruce purchase a summer home. They each have families and so would like to own the property in such a way that if either died, his family could continue to use and enjoy the property. If they take title as tenants in common, their objectives will be accomplished, for on the death of either Bruce or Bernard, the deceased brother's share will pass through his estate. If he leaves the property to his family, they will be the new tenants in common with the surviving brother and may continue to use and own the deceased brother's share of the property. On the other hand, if Bruce and Bernard took title as joint tenants with rights of survivorship, the death of either brother would terminate the deceased brother's rights to the property and the surviving brother would own the property in full. The family of the deceased brother would have no rights to the property (at least not without a fight).

Another essential difference between a tenancy in common and a joint tenancy is the respective shares of the co-tenants. With a joint tenancy, all the co-tenants must have *equal* (undivided) shares, whereas with a tenancy in common the share of each co-tenancy may be different. For example, one person may have a 10 percent interest in property as a tenant in common with another person who has the remaining 90 percent interest. Any difference in interest between the co-tenants, however, does not affect each co-tenant's right to possession of the property.

CREATION OF TENANCY IN COMMON

A TENANCY IN COMMON MAY BE created voluntarily or involuntarily, that is, intentionally or by accident. It can be the result of an agreement, it can be created by law, by a bequest under a will, or by error or mistake in attempting to create another form of co-tenancy, such as a joint tenancy or a tenancy by the entirety; it can also be created by a transfer of property to two or more persons, where there is no mention of survivorship rights or of the type of co-tenancy desired.

BY AGREEMENT OF THE CO-TENANTS

If the tenancy in common is created by agreement or by a voluntary act of the parties, it should, like any desired legal objective, be carefully spelled out. Failure to do so will merely bring about costly delays and legal battles later on. For example, in our hypothetical situation above, Bruce and Bernard should be sure the language of the deed to their new summer home clearly indicates a tenancy in common. It could say " . . . to Bruce Boundary, An undivided one-half interest, and to Bernard Boundary, An undivided one-half interest, *as tenants in common and not as joint tenants . . . .*" But this language is not for universal use. Each deed must be drafted separately to fit the particular circumstances and state law. Any such deed and the necessary language should of course be prepared by an attorney who is made aware of the desires and objectives of the parties. It is the home-drawn deed that more often contains the ambiguities and conflicting provisions that lead to complications and court cases.

If the property involved is *personal* property as opposed to real estate, a formal deed does not always accompany the transfer to the co-tenants. Personal property is generally any property *except* real estate. It includes, for example, automobiles, furnishings, machinery, jewelry, etc. (these would be considered tangible personal property), and bank accounts, stocks, bonds, copyrights, etc. (these would be considered *in*tangible personal property). Sales or transfers of personal property are usually accompanied by a bill of sale or other statement. If a bill of sale or similar document is given, the document should contain the necessary language properly creating the tenancy in common or the joint tenancy, whichever is desired. If no documentation accompanies the transfer, the parties should have some written agreement or acknowledgment stating their intent as to how the property is held, whether it be a joint tenancy or a tenancy in common, and if a tenancy in common, whether the shares are equal or not.

When the property is a bank account or securities, a written statement or agreement is almost always essential. For bank accounts, the bank signature cards are not always enough, especially if a tenancy in common is desired. Some additional written statement is needed. When securities are involved, fewer problems generally exist because most security transfer agents clearly indicate the nature of ownership on the certificate itself.

Nevertheless, it would not hurt to confirm this by some outside agreement or statement indicating the intent of the parties.

The communication need not be very formal, a simple letter or memorandum signed by each of the co-tenants would usually suffice. A simple example of the type of communication I am suggesting might be (for two owners) as follows: "With respect to the bank account numbered 1234 in our names at the Last National Bank of Boston, this is to state it is our understanding and agreement that the funds in that account belong one-half to each of us and that on the death of either of us, one-half the funds existing in said account on that date will belong to the survivor and the other half will pass to the estate of the one deceased." (This language would, of course, indicate a *tenancy in common*; for a statement of intent indicating a *joint tenancy* see Chapter 7.) In either case, the statement, letter, or agreement should be signed by *each* of the co-tenants to indicate his or her acknowledgment. Furthermore, it is *essential* that the language and objectives of the co-tenants be consistent with the language and effect of other legal documents they may have, such as a will or trust. If the statement says one thing and the will or trust another, we may be back where we started.

BY LAW

Certain transactions and occurrences may automatically leave the parties as tenants in common, even though their relationship prior to the transaction or occurrence was as joint tenants or otherwise.

If partners operating a business purchase property for business use, they will own the property in what amounts to a tenancy in common in proportion to their respective shares of the partnership, unless stated otherwise.

When a married couple who owned property as tenants by the entirety become divorced, the tenancy by the entirety is—in most states—terminated and they will own the property as tenants in common (see Chapter 4). A similar result will occur after divorce in a community property state where community property is not disposed of by the divorce decree.

And where a court judgment is obtained as the result of a lawsuit and the successful party seizes joint property of which the unsuccessful party is a joint owner, the seizure can convert the joint tenancy into a tenancy in common.

A tenancy in common can be achieved inadvertently when a transfer of property is made to two or more persons without indicating whether they are to be joint tenants or tenants in common. For example, George transfers his summer home to his wife, Georgette, and his daughter, Georgia, the deed transferring the property merely stating "to Georgette and Georgia . . . ." In such a case, there is a *presumption* that Georgette and Georgia take the property *as tenants in common and not as joint tenants*. This presumption is established in most states by law, since so much confusion was generated from the old common law presumption, which was just the opposite. So, if a joint tenancy with rights of survivorship is desired, it must be *specifically* and clearly stated.

A bequest in a will can often have the same effect as a transfer to two or more persons as discussed above. That is, unless the intent clearly indicates a joint tenancy, a tenancy in common will be created when a person leaves property to two or more beneficiaries. So that if Uncle Fred says in his will, "I leave my estate to my nephew, Carl, and his wife, Helen . . . " then Carl and Helen will take Uncle Fred's property as tenants in common and *not* as joint tenants, since it was not so specified by Uncle Fred in his will.

Although this presumption that a transfer to two or more persons creates a tenancy in common may be simply stated, its effect on a family can be complicted and unexpected. In the case of Patrick Cross, for example, it took review by two courts to finally decide the issue. Patrick died in 1928. In his will he left the bulk of his estate "to my son Thomas . . . and to my son William . . . share and share alike." In 1933 son William died (without a will) leaving a wife and two children, and seven years later, son Thomas died leaving his share to his four children. On the theory that a joint tenancy had been created by Patrick, Thomas' family claimed the entire property since Thomas survived William. On the theory that Patrick had created a tenancy in common between Thomas and William, William's family claimed its one-half share.

The lower court held in favor of William's family and ordered the property divided. The Massachusetts Supreme Judicial Court reviewed Patrick's will once again and *examined the records and testimony to try to determine Patrick's intent.* Did he want Thomas and William to take as joint tenants so that if either died, the deceased brother's share would pass to the surviving brother? The Supreme Court could find no evidence indicating an intent that the sons take as joint tenants, and therefore applied the established law which provides that Patrick's bequest to his sons, including the words "share and share alike," *created a tenancy in common,* and that both families were entitled to an equal share. Once again, the lack of a clear expression of intent caused family bitterness, as well as delays and expenses for everyone involved.

BY TRANSFER

A tenancy in common can also be created out of a joint tenancy when a joint tenant transfers his interest to a third party. For example, Robert and Richard own property as joint tenants with rights of survivorship, and Richard sells his undivided share to Donald. The joint tenancy between Robert and Richard would no longer exist. Robert would now be a tenant in common with Donald. However, if Richard and Donald wanted to be joint tenants, they could do so by agreement or by a new transfer to themselves as joint tenants with rights of survivorship. (In some states this must be done through a transfer to a "straw" who, in turn, transfers the property immediately back to the parties, as joint tenants.)

CREATION BY MISTAKE

Perhaps the most dangerous way to create a tenancy in common is by mistake, since the results are generally not what the parties themselves intended when creating the co-tenancy. Often a parent will transfer property to two or more children with the intent that if one child died, the surviving child or children would automatically take the property. If the proper wording is not used or if it is even left out by accident in the process of preparing the transfer deed, it could result in a tenancy in common rather than a joint tenancy. More often than not it is the lack of proper wording rather than accidental omissions that produces unexpected results. The case of Nick Kijurina is a good illustration of this.

Sarah Jaic and Nick Kijurina lived together as husband and wife for eighteen years. In fact, Sarah came to be known as Sarah Kijurina. But they were never married because Sarah's actual husband, Laso Jaic, had deserted her and she was never able to obtain a divorce.

In 1935 they purchased a home in Westmoreland County, Pennsylvania, and the property was deeded to them as "Nick Kijurina and Sarah, his wife." Sometime later, Sarah died. In her will, Sarah left her share of the home as well as all of her personal property to her sister, her brother-in-law, her nephew and niece. Her sister, Mary Teacher, was appointed executrix under Sarah's will and made claim to Sarah's share of the real estate, on the basis that Sarah, as a *tenant in common* with Nick, had a right to leave her share to someone else, namely Mary and the others. Nick, totally astounded by the claim against the property that he felt he owned, and which was purchased with his money, and which, in any event, was (he felt) *jointly* owned by Sarah and himself, rebuffed Mary's claims out of hand. Mary sued.

In the meantime, Nick had taken a new wife, then died a year later, leaving his entire estate to his new wife, Julia. So Mary sued Julia. And so did Sarah's brother-in-law, and Sarah's niece and nephew. After hearing testimony regarding the intent of the deceased parties (Sarah and Nick) and the contributions made by each to the purchase of the property (it was Nick's money), the lower court found that a joint tenancy was intended, and therefore Nick was entitled to a survivorship interest in the property, which in turn meant that Julia was entitled to it.

An appeal was taken to the Supreme Court of Pennsylvania where the issues turned out to be a little more complicated, turning on the question of the type of interest given to a "married" couple who were, in fact, not married. Under common law, a joint tenancy could be construed in such a case. However, by the Act of 1812 Pennsylvania abolished the "incident of survivorship" and established a law requiring that *a survivorship interest must "clearly appear" in order to overcome the presumption against it.* In this case, said the Supreme Court, the words "Nick Kijurina and Sarah, his wife," without more, did *not* clearly create a survivorship interest, and Sarah was held to have possessed a one-half interest in the home as a tenant in common, which interest could be passed on to her estate!

One might speculate in this case that since Sarah was Nick's wife for more than eighteen years and Julia just over a year, and since neither marriage produced children, it was only equitable for Sarah's heirs to receive a fair share. To produce this more equitable result, the court need only find the evidence insufficient to prove the required "intent." However, this is pure speculation; the fact remains that the wording of the deed was poor in the first place and the litigation could most likely have been avoided with the addition of a few simple words clarifying the intent of the original owners.

TYPE OF PROPERTY

A TENANCY IN COMMON MAY exist in virtually every species of property, in all types of real estate, and in all types of personal property such as jewelry, motor vehicles, boats, crops, bank accounts, stocks and bonds, leases, and livestock; even cemetery plots. The tenancy may come into existence gradually, as when crops are planted and later considered to be grown, or with "growing" livestock, as in the case of Mr. Hollis and Mr. York. In that case, Hollis owned eighty-five hogs which needed to be fattened before sale. He entered into an agreement with Mr. York, who had an ungathered peanut crop on his land, whereby York would take Hollis' hogs and would care for and fatten them on his peanut crop. The hogs were weighed when given to York and it was agreed that when the hogs were sold, Hollis would be paid for their initial weight plus one-half of the weight gained, and York would be paid for one-half of the weight gained. In effect, they were (equal) tenants in common with respect to the total weight gained by the hogs.

Other property may unknowingly be the subject of a tenancy in common, such as a tree growing exactly on the boundary line between two parcels of adjoining land. The owners of the abutting parcels are tenants in common, each owning an undivided one-half interest in the tree on the boundary line. It is even possible to have a tenancy in common with a dead person with property such as a cemetery lot. Some cases dealing with co-tenants' rights to cemetery lots illustrate an important, but in this particular case undesirable, aspect of the tenancy in common—the right to possession.

In August 1899 Frank Silva purchased a cemetery lot in the Pocasset Hill Cemetery, in Tiverton, Rhode Island. It was his intention that he and his children would be buried there. On his death, Frank left the property to his children as tenants in common. Sometime in April 1946 the grandchild of Mary Helger, one of Frank's daughters, met an untimely death. Mary had the grandchild buried in the lot her father Frank had left her. Because the remaining children felt strongly about preserving the cemetery lot for family members, namely Frank's children, they objected to Mary about the burial, and later brought legal action to have the child's body removed from the lot.

The court acknowledged that generally a tenant in common may make any reasonable use of the land, so long as it does not result in an exclusion of the other tenants from enjoying their equal privileges. However, in the case of a cemetery lot that has been purchased for family burial, the consent of all the co-tenants is required, because if other parties are buried in the place of family members, the remaining family members would still have a right of "possession" based on the order of their deaths, and there may not be enough room for the last of the family members to die.

In this case, one of the Silva children could conceivably be deprived of a burial space because of the presence of the child's body in his lot. Although Mary had a right to place her grandchild's body in the lot, she did not have the right to deprive the other tenants in common (her brothers and sisters) of the right to possession of their respective shares of the lot at death, which could happen if Mary herself were also buried there.

On the other hand, the court said, the policy of the law is, except in case of necessity, that the sanctity of the grave should be maintained, and a body once suitably buried should not be disturbed. They felt that although the rights of the remaining Silva children could be affected, the child's body should not be removed. It was decided then that the proper resolution would be to treat the failure of Mary to remove her grandchild's body as an election by Mary to let the grandchild lie buried there in Mary's place, and that unless Mary had the consent of all her brothers and sisters, Mary would thereby forgo the right to be buried there herself. In other words, she would give up her right to possession, in effect having made the grandchild a tenant in common in her place.

Although the concept of burial lots is somewhat unique, this case nevertheless illustrates two points important to a tenancy in common. Even though each tenant in common may use or even transfer his or her share of the property as he or she sees fit, the right to possession is always present. This right may be enjoyed by each co-tenant, but not to the exclusion of the others, and to protect or enforce that right a court may order certain action to be taken, such as the removal of a body, a building, or a tree, in the interests of equity. Second, in a tenancy in common, as with any co-tenancy, the co-tenants may all agree on a particular use for the property, and if agreed to, such use may be binding not only on the co-tenants, but also on anyone taking or inheriting a co-tenant's share.

TERMINATION OF A TENANCY IN COMMON

BECAUSE A RIGHT TO possession of the property by all the co-tenants is essential to a tenancy in common, anything that severs or destroys that right will terminate the tenancy in common.

Therefore, if the property is *actually divided* between or among the co-tenants, the tenancy in common will be terminated, or if the property is *abandoned,* the tenancy will likewise be terminated. If both or all the co-tenants *transfer* the property to a stranger or third person, the co-tenancy as to that property will be terminated, but one will still exist in the proceeds of the transfer until they are divided.

Division of the proceeds or of the property itself is one of the easiest ways to terminate a tenancy in common. The general rule, however, is that property held as a tenancy in common cannot be divided unless all the owners agree or unless ordered by a court, but this rule applies only to property that is not easily and reasonably divisible or that consists of a single object that cannot be divided without destroying its nature or individuality, such as a house or painting. When the property is easily divisible and of the same quality and characteristic throughout, such as a load of coal or a barrel of whiskey, each tenant may take his share (but *only* his share) without the consent of the others. This point is well illustrated in the case of Jane Dickey.

Jane Dickey and Sam Spears owned land in Greenup County, Kentucky, as tenants in common. An iron furnace was operated on the land for many years causing the buildup of an immense pile of cinders or slag on the property. The accumulation, which was anywhere from six to twenty feet deep and covered about two acres of land, was so great that in 1887 they thought they would abandon the land, since no one felt there was or would be any value as it stood and certainly the cinders were of no use. In later years, however, it was discovered that cinders could be quite useful in foundations for highways. Upon learning this, Sam, without consulting Jane, negotiated with the Kentucky State Highway Commission for the use of the cinders in the construction of a state road in the vicinity, and the Highway Commission removed several thousand cubic yards of cinders before Jane found out about the deal. Jane brought suit against Sam to recover damages of one-half the value of the removed cinders.

The Kentucky Court of Appeals observed that less than one-half of the total volume of cinders was removed by Sam Spear, and that so long as Mrs. Dickey's one-half of the cinders was not disturbed or threatened, she had no right to sue. It went on to recite the rule that personal property that is severable by nature may be taken by a co-tenant (up to his share) without the consent of the others, but such a taking will terminate the co-tenancy as to that property taken. Sam owed nothing to Jane except to take no more than his one-half of the cinders.

It should be noted that an actual, physical separation of property or shares is required for the type of termination discussed above. The mere preparation to divide or the decision as to what method will be used to divide the property is not enough.

Occasionally, a co-tenant may desire to terminate tenancy in common but cannot. For example, say that two parties agree to purchase property as tenants in common, one pays the purchase price and then can't get reimbursed by the other. Can the purchasing party oust the other? Probably not. That's what happened in the case of James Anderson. He and Charles Snowden agreed to buy land as tenants in common. Snowden did not have the funds so Anderson put up all the money. After repeated requests, Snowden still could not come up with the cash. The land appreciated in value and Anderson decided that he should be the sole owner. He told Snowden that if he did not come up with the funds by a certain date, he (Anderson) would consider the property entirely his and refuse to recognize any ownership by Snowden. The date passed without payment and Anderson went to court to have the property declared legally his.

The court held that the tenancy in common arose by agreement *and* by the deed conveying the property. Anderson could not by himself force a forfeiture or termination; Snowden was entitled to a one-half interest in the property on payment of one-half the purchase price with interest and expenses. It was not clear how long a period of time Snowden would have to come up with the money. Could he wait until the land was sold, then just offset his costs with his share of the proceeds? Maybe. Although it doesn't seem fair to Anderson, it appears that just as "a rose is a rose," so a co-tenancy is a co-tenancy, and each co-tenant should be aware of his rights to the commonly held property. One point is clear in cases like this: each tenant should bear his share of the costs at the time of purchase to avoid such a confrontation.

SUMMARY

A KNOWLEDGE OF THE elements of *tenancy in common* is important to any consideration of a *joint tenancy,* even though they differ, because a joint tenancy may be converted to a tenancy in common, sometimes voluntarily, sometimes involuntarily. A tenancy in common may be created by agreement, by law, or by accident or mistake. The primary difference between a joint tenancy and a tenancy in common is the right of survivorship, which exists in the joint tenancy but is *absent* in the tenancy in common; the tenant in common "keeps" his or her share even after death—that is, it passes to the deceased co-tenant's estate. As in the joint tenancy, problems arise with the tenancy in common largely as a result of incorrect use of language in documents, questions of intent of the co-tenants with lack of any tangible proof of intent, and misunderstanding of the nature of a co-tenancy. Such problems can be avoided by understanding the rights of each co-tenant and by a clear expression of the intent of the parties with respect to the commonly held property.

4

TENANCY BY THE ENTIRETY

ONE OF THE FEW THINGS THAT just about every married couple seems to agree upon is that their home should be held by them in a way that will allow the survivor to own and enjoy the property if either should die—what they usually understand to be a joint tenancy. More often than not, however, the property is not held by the husband and wife *jointly* but rather as *tenants by the entirety.*

Is this the same as a joint tenancy? Which method of ownership is preferable? Why is the tenancy by the entirety so popular?

BASICS OF THE TENANCY BY THE ENTIRETY— WHAT IT IS

A TENANCY BY THE ENTIRETY is a *special form of joint tenancy* which may be used *only* by a husband and wife. It originated under the English common law when property was transferred to husband and wife together, and the nature of their rights had to be established. In early days, the unity of man and woman by marriage was, for legal purposes, actually treated as a unification of the two people, so that their ownership of property (usually real estate) was not regarded as being owned by the two, but by the "unity," or by the "entirety." The whole of the property is owned not by the two people but rather by the unity created when the parties were married; the two took title as a single person. Under the common law legal principles the existence of the wife, for legal purposes, was merged with that of her husband. During the term of the marriage her legal identity was "suspended." From this legal viewpoint, the two became one and that one was the husband—hence the tenancy by "one" or "by the entirety." Even though modern attitudes (and laws) regarding property ownership and the rights of women reflect the equality of men and women, the deep-seated roots of the tenancy by the entirety remain in many states, and as a form of ownership it is still popular.

Because of this entirety concept, neither party, acting alone, could transfer his or her interest in the property held by the entirety, and on the death of either party, the survivor would own the whole property (in this respect similar to a joint tenancy). It would remain this way until both agreed to a transfer or until the marriage was dissolved by law or by the death of one of the parties. *Note:* Since the tenancy by the entirety is basically a creature of English common law, the various states have developed their own interpretations of this form of ownership. The concept and elements discussed here reflect the common law principles as well as the position of a large number of states, but do not necessarily apply to every state. Presently, twenty-four jurisdictions still recognize the tenancy by the entirety in some form.[1] Many states, however, have actually abolished tenancy by the entirety on the theory that it is outmoded and does not reflect the present-day attitude that husband and wife are individuals, notwithstanding their marriage relationship. Generally speaking, however, any law that abolishes the tenancy by the entirety will be prospective rather than retroactive, so that existing tenancies may stand if the parties so wish.

Furthermore, in some states a tenancy by the entirety may result even though title to the particular account or other property may actually use the words "joint tenants." In those states that recognize the tenancy by the entirety, there is often a presumption that when husband and wife take property as joint tenants, they are actually taking as tenants by the entirety. To eliminate this presumption (if this is what is desired), the title should read "as joint tenants and not as tenants by the entirety." In any event the presumption in any given state should be determined if there is a question, and careful attention should be paid to the distinctions between the two forms of ownership.

Some states that still recognize tenancy by the entirety have adopted a Married Women's Act, which legally recognizes the individuality of women and which, at first glance, seems to conflict with certain concepts of the tenancy by the entirety. Still other states are "community property" states[2] where property acquired during marriage belongs equally to both spouses, and where a tenancy by the entirety created in such states will have no effect on the disposition of property owned by the husband and wife. It is important, therefore, to keep in mind that the material in this chapter is but a guide to understanding the nature of the tenancy by the entirety, where it may apply.

HOW IT WORKS

THE TENANCY BY THE ENTIRETY is somewhat like a joint tenancy in that there is a right of survivorship in both. That is, on the death of either owner, the survivor will own the whole property. However, there are other factors which distinguish the tenancy by the entirety from the joint tenancy: a joint tenancy may be held by any number of persons, while a tenancy by the entirety may be held *only* by husband and wife. A joint tenancy may be severed or terminated by an act of any one of the joint tenants, while a tenancy by the entirety may not be transferred unless *both* parties agree, and may not be severed (divided) except by court or legal action, or by agreement of both husband and wife.

The right of a surviving spouse to own the whole property on the death of a spouse is one of the advantages of holding property by the entirety. Such property passing to a surviving spouse becomes hers or his alone without passing through probate (a state's legal procedure required to settle a deceased person's estate—see Chapter 12), and without being subject to the claims of creditors of the deceased person (unless the property itself was pledged as collateral or security, such as a mortgage signed by both parties). The surviving spouse may then dispose of the property as her or his own, regardless of any provision to the contrary in the will of the deceased spouse.

If both spouses died at the same time (called a simultaneous death as discussed in Chapter 1) the property would be distributed as if they owned it as tenants in common. In other words, one-half the property would pass through the husband's estate and one-half through the wife's estate.

It is possible to combine different forms of co-tenancy; they are not always mutually exclusive. For example, a husband and wife could own a share of property as tenants by the entirety with another person as tenants in common. This is what happened in the Lucas case.

In 1941 the Lucas family purchased a farm in Washington County, Pennsylvania. Title was given to them in the names of "Joseph Lucas and Matilda Lucas, his wife, and Francis Lucas, a single man." Francis was the son of Joseph and Matilda. In September 1949 Joseph died and one M. W. Heather, a creditor of Joseph, brought suit against Joseph's estate to collect funds he felt Joseph owed to him. Because Joseph had an interest in the farm, Heather asked the court to order the farm sold to satisfy his claim out of Joseph's one-third share. The question was, did Joseph have a one-third share that could be sold?

In reviewing the facts and the deed the court decided that the property was owned in *two shares* under a tenancy in common: one tenant in common was the son, Francis, and the other was Joseph and Matilda. However, the share of the tenancy in common owned by Joseph and Matilda was owned by them as a tenancy by the entirety, so that on the death of either, the survivor would own the whole share as a tenant in common with the son, Francis. Because Joseph and Matilda's share was considered by the court a tenancy by the entirety, Joseph's share was not subject to sale by Heather; it automatically passed to Matilda free of Heather's claim, and Matilda was allowed to keep her share of the farm.

Even though property held under a tenancy by the entirety may be sold or exchanged, the character of the ownership will generally follow the proceeds of the newly acquired property. For example, if husband and wife sell their home which is held in a tenancy by the entirety and place the proceeds in a bank account, the bank account may be also held as a tenancy by the entirety, as can the property that is later purchased with those funds. Of course, the parties could divide the proceeds or agree to take new title in a form other than a tenancy by the entirety, in which case the tenancy by the entirety would be terminated.

HOW IS A TENANCY BY THE ENTIRETY CREATED?

IN THOSE STATES THAT recognize the existence of a tenancy by the entirety, this type of ownership may be created by a transfer of property to husband and wife, even though the instrument of transfer does not state how they are to take it. Under the common law concept, the tenancy by the entirety was *presumed* since this was the basic form of ownership for husband and wife. For example, Edgar sells his land to Carl and Carol (who are married) and Edgar's deed to them says only: "To Carl and Carol Carlson, husband and wife." In this case, they will be presumed to take the property as tenants by the entirety. As a general rule, however, it is always best to state the manner in which title is intended, to eliminate any question of intent. And remember, if property is transferred to husband and wife without stating more, in a state where tenancy by the entirety is *not* recognized, they will take the property as *tenants in common,* and *no survivorship right will exist.* If this is casually overlooked, it could bring about a big disappointment for a surviving spouse. As in all forms of co-tenancies, the words creating the co-tenancies are vital to the transaction. If words are used that clearly indicate a joint tenancy between husband and wife, that is what will be created, rather than a tenancy by the entirety, as Daniel Wiggens sadly found out. Daniel and his wife, Laura Belle Wiggens, were granted a parcel of land in Randolph County, Indiana, in December 1884. The deed transferred the property "To Daniel S. Wiggens and Laura Belle Wiggens, his wife, in *joint tenancy* . . . ." One of Daniel's creditors, William Thornbury, sued Daniel, and being successful, he then tried to have Daniel's one-half of the jointly held property sold to satisfy his claim. Daniel argued that since the property was held by himself and his wife as tenants by the entirety they held as "one," and their interests could not be divided; the land should not be sold.

The question was, did they in fact hold the property as tenants by the entirety? Isn't there a presumption that as husband and wife they would take as tenants by the entirety? The court observed that such a presumption would occur when the intent of the transfer was *vague,* but here the language in the deed clearly stated "in joint tenancy," and joint tenants they would be. Therefore, Daniel's share of one-half the jointly held property was subject to the court order that it be *sold* to satisfy Thornbury's claim.

Then, of course, there are cases where the deed specifically states "tenants by the entirety," but where the parties, or one of them, wanted something else. In such a case, is a tenancy by the entirety created? Once again, the *intent* of the transaction is critical, as Betty Huss discovered.

After deciding they could no longer remain married, James and Betty Huss obtained a divorce. During their marriage, however, James had purchased a tract of land in Gaston County, North Carolina, with his own funds. Title to the property was in the names of James and Betty "as tenants by the entirety." Since they were now divorced, Betty brought an action in court asking that the property be ordered sold so that she could have her share.

James, in his answer to Betty's claim, said the whole thing was a mistake. That is, when he bought the land in 1962 in instructed the people who sold it to him that he wanted the property in his name alone. At the actual transfer, he didn't think to look at the deed, since the sellers assured him it was as he requested it. In fact, he learned of the mistake only when Betty sought relief in court. James therefore asked the court not to order the property sold but rather to order it placed in his name alone to rectify the mistake.

The Court of Appeals believed James and dismissed Betty's claim. In reading the official report on the case, it is difficult to tell whether there really was a mistake; James offered nothing to prove it except his assertions of the misunderstanding! Nevertheless, the court deemed this sufficient and Betty lost her claim to a share of the house. The facts of this case may not be typical, but one aspect of it is: words aren't always what they seem to be, especially when a co-tenancy is under attack. The courts will look into, under, and around the words to determine the true *intent of the parties* and to arrive at an equitable resolution of the dispute. In doing so they may apply statutory law, common law, or just plain common sense.

In following the common law, creation of a tenancy by the entirety involves certain legal requirements that must be present to have a valid tenancy. One of these requirements is that the husband and wife acquire their respective interests in the property at the *same time* and under the same deed of transfer. In other words, a transfer to the husband who later transfers the same property to himself and his wife as tenants by the entirety would *not* meet the legal requirements under the common law, since he acquired title at one time and she at another.

Although some states have substantially relaxed these requirements, other states that recognize the tenancy by the entirety generally still require them. There is little consistency in this aspect of the law. This requirement may pose a problem when one spouse, say the husband, purchases the property in his own name either prior to or after the marriage, then wishes to transfer the property to himself and his wife as tenants by the entirety, as previously suggested. In some states this cannot be done. If the husband takes his title from one person (the seller) and the wife takes her title from her husband, there is no "unity of title." Therefore, in those states where a statute has not been enacted that allows the spouses to create a tenancy by the entirety in this fashion, the husband must transfer the property to a "straw." (A straw is usually an individual who has no true interest in the transaction but merely acts where another person is needed.) Here the husband would transfer the property to a straw, who in turn would immediately transfer the property back to the husband and wife as tenants by the entirety. Since they received their title from the same deed (the straw's deed) there would now be a unity of title, which would validate the tenancy by the entirety.

MARRIED OR NOT

CREATION AND EXISTENCE OF the tenancy by the entirety does not depend upon the parties living together, and there are no requirements that there be love and affection between them or that they remain faithful to one another, only that they be married. Once created, the tenancy depends entirely on the marital status and continues until death or divorce. This means that a husband and wife who lived apart because they couldn't stand one another, and who while living apart were unfaithful to one another, could still enjoy the advantages of a tenancy by the entirety—while another couple, unmarried but living together for years and very happy with each other, could *not,* as Alice Coleman discovered after the death of her paramour, Tom Jackson.

Alice and Tom lived together in Washington, D.C., as man and wife from 1926 until Tom's death in 1957. During that time they had eleven children but were *never legally married.* Although Alice Coleman became known as Alice Jackson, Tom was still legally married to Susie Jackson, whom he had married in 1903. (Tom also had two children by Susie.)

In 1952 Tom and Alice purchased some real estate and the deed to the property stated that it was transferred to "Thomas H. Jackson and wife, Alice W. Jackson . . . as Tenants by the Entirety." After Tom died, Alice treated the entire property as hers and later sold it. Tom's legitimate wife, Susie, and his children (by Susie) brought legal action against Alice to recover Tom's share of the proceeds of the sale. Their argument was that because Tom and Alice were not legally married they could not have taken the real estate as tenants by the entirety. Therefore, they took as tenants in common, and since he left no will, Tom's share should pass to his legal heirs. (Susie and her children were Tom's legal heirs; Alice and the eleven illegitimate children were not.)

Alice, on the other hand, claimed that although a tenancy by the entirety may not have been created, she was still entitled to survivorship interest in the property, as this was their intent.

The District Court agreed with Susie and her children and ordered Alice to pay Tom's share to them. Alice appealed.

The Appeals Court agreed that when property is transferred to two or more persons (including husband and wife) a tenancy in common is presumed, unless expressly declared otherwise. However, even though Alice and Tom were not husband and wife and therefore could not take as tenants by the entirety, the facts were clear that they *intended* a survivorship interest. So the court declared that Alice was a surviving joint tenant of the property and she was allowed to keep the proceeds of the sale of that property.

Once again, confusion, costly litigation, and bitterness occur because of a few incorrect words in a deed in an attempt to create a "simple" tenancy by the entirety.

A case somewhat similar to that of Tom and Alice Jackson was that of Michael and Mabel Bove. Michael Bove began living with Mabel (Bender) Bove in 1926. During the years that followed Mable bore him two children but Michael and Mabel were never married. Mabel was the lawful wife of one Frank Bender until he gave her a divorce in 1948, twenty-two years after she began living with Michael.

Prior to Mabel's divorce, that is, while she was still legally married to Frank, Michael purchased some real estate, which was subsequently transferred to his and Mabel's names "as tenants by the entirety." On Michael's death, his executor, John Bove, brought an action to eject Mabel from the property, on the basis that they could not have held as tenants by the entirety since they were not married and therefore not eligible to hold title in this way. The result, they argued, was that a tenancy in common was created. Mabel countered that even though the tenancy by the entirety was unavailable to them, their *intent* was to create a survivorship interest and this should not be defeated just because they weren't married. The court agreed with Mabel. Applying the same reasoning as in the Jackson case, the court held that the parties intended a survivorship interest and therefore a joint tenancy was created.

As illustrated in these cases, the courts generally attempt to resolve ambiguous situations in a manner satisfying the apparent intent of the parties. This is, however, leaving a great deal to chance and to the amount of evidence that may be available to show the parties' intent. Often it is only the language in the deed that is available. There is a better way: document your intent; make sure that you understand the form of ownership that you have and that you have met the legal requirements, if any, and seek proper professional guidance on the transaction.

THE HUSBAND'S RIGHT TO POSSESSION

AS PREVIOUSLY POINTED OUT, the tenancy by the entirety derives from the early common law concept of the unity of marriage. When a couple married they became one in the eyes of the law, and that "one" was the husband. He, therefore, was entitled to exclusive control and possession of the property during his life. The wife had a right to the property only if she survived her husband. During their joint lives, however, neither spouse acting alone could defeat the other's interest in the property. They would be required to act together on any sale or other transfer until the marriage was dissolved. The act of either one alone was ineffective in transferring the property. Further, in addition to possession, if the property produced any income or profits, the husband was exclusively entitled to this as well.

These concepts have been somewhat modified in recent years. Many states have enacted Married Women's Acts or similar statutes, which may abolish the husband's exclusive right to possession and profits, and equalize the rights between the spouses. Still other states have abolished altogether the tenancy by the entirety, so that a joint tenancy with rights of survivorship is often the next choice. If a question arises, the law of the particular state involved should be carefully examined before settling upon a specific form of ownership.

MAY A TENANCY BY THE ENTIRETY EXIST IN OWNERSHIP OF PERSONAL PROPERTY?

A TENANCY BY THE ENTIRETY IS not necessarily restricted to real estate; in many states it may also exist in ownership of personal property. Personal property may generally be regarded as all property other than real estate and may be divided into two major categories: *tangible* personal property and *intangible* personal property.

Examples of tangible personal property would be furniture, jewelry, automobiles, clothing, and items that can be touched. Intangible personal property, on the other hand, refers more to property rights than physical property, and includes, for example, such things as stock certificates, bank accounts, or the right to sue someone. Actual cash is usually considered tangible personal property.

Under very early English common law, a tenancy by the entirety in personal property was generally considered an impossibility since any personal property of the wife became at once the property of the husband because of the "unity" concept of marriage. This inequity, however, has been removed by the modern Married Women's Acts. Present-day legal attitudes toward this type of tenancy in personal property depend almost exclusively on the law of the particular state in question. That is, some states, such as Massachusetts, Arkansas, Mississippi, and Delaware, have recognized the existence of such a tenancy in personal property, while others such as Oregon, Missouri, and New Jersey have abolished such tenancies by law, and even when one is desired, it cannot be used. One thing is clear, that the several states are not consistent on this point. It does appear, however, that the majority of states will recognize a tenancy by the entirety in personal property.

In those states that recognize a tenancy by the entirety in personal property it can be quite useful when household goods are concerned. Very often, a husband and wife will overlook disposition of household goods that may have substantial value. Antiques, oriental rugs, family heirlooms, and even used furniture may be the subject of a dispute among the surviving spouse and other family members if its disposition on the death of a spouse is not clear. If it can be established that such property was jointly held or held under a tenancy by the entirety, a good deal of trouble and expense may be avoided. Tennessee and Pennsylvania courts have held that documenting evidence is not necessary to establish a tenancy by the entirety in household goods, and that there is a fair presumption that where household goods are in the joint possession of husband and wife living together, the title of the goods is in the parties as tenants by the entirety, so that on the husband's death the property belongs to the wife and not to the estate.

Title to such property, however, should not be left to chance. Where the ownership of household goods is important to a married couple (and it should always be, since the survivor would have no less a need to use the property), the couple should document their ownership. A simple written declaration by the couple should suffice, stating that the goods were purchased by them for their joint use and that on the death of either, the survivor will be the absolute owner. But this approach should not be used arbitrarily, especially if the property is of substantial value, since, as will be seen in Chapter 10 on taxes, too much joint property can have an expensive effect on your estate plan.

If there is any specific property that either spouse should want to maintain as his or her own, that should be expressly excluded from any written declaration. It should be noted that a joint declaration could be a problem if the couple should later obtain a divorce. Property that was originally the property of one spouse would now be jointly held and most likely divided in a divorce settlement. Nevertheless, it is a reasonable risk to take to insure the convenience of a survivorship interest in the household property.

LIABILITY FOR A SPOUSE'S DEBTS

EVERYONE WOULD LIKE TO FEEL his or her property is insulated against claims of creditors, and many go to great lengths to do so. Lots of people are under the impression that property held as a tenancy by the entirety offers such insulation; the fact is that it may, but then again it may not. For the most part, it depends upon whether the creditors are creditors of husband or wife, or both, and most importantly, whether the state you're in happens to recognize tenancy by the entirety and what the state's position is on creditor's rights to such property.

Generally speaking, if a husband and wife are *jointly* liable on a debt, that is, if they both sign the promissory note and/or both agree to pay the debt, then any property they own, whether individually, jointly, or as tenants by the entirety, may be subject to attachment (seizure by legal process) and sale for nonpayment of the debt. On the other hand, if the debt is an individual one of the husband or of the wife, then property they hold as tenants by the entirety is usually not subject to sale to satisfy the debt.

The case of Abraham Gluskin is a good example of this. Abraham and his wife owned a tract of land in Springfield, Massachusetts, as tenants by the entirety. A creditor of Abraham's wife (and not of Abraham) attached the property through a lawsuit and was successful in winning the suit. To satisfy the judgment against the wife, the creditor asked that a sheriff's sale of the property be carried out so his claim could be satisfied. Abraham brought suit to prevent the sale.

The Massachusetts Supreme Judicial Court took notice of the fact that the Gluskins' property was held under a tenancy by the entirety. As such, the property could not be sold or transferred by either the husband or the wife acting alone, and that even if either tried to transfer the property, he or she could not defeat the right of the survivor to take the entire property on the death of the other. If this is the law, the court said, why should a creditor be able to do that which an owner of the property himself cannot do. Since the wife cannot sell it herself, the creditor cannot sell it, even through the court. The creditor's order for sale was rescinded and the Gluskins kept the property.

Of course, if the property is pledged as security for the note (such as on a mortgage), that property may clearly be sold to satisfy nonpayment of the debt. For example, in the usual case husband and wife purchase a home and finance a part of the purchase price through a bank or other lending institution. The lender will have both husband and wife sign the note (even if only one of them is working), and they will also be required to give the lender a mortgage on the property. (A mortgage is an actual transfer of an interest in the real estate to secure the payment of the note.) If the lender did not do this, it might not be able to sell the property to recover the loan (on default) if the property was held under a tenancy by the entirety.

The reason for this apparent insulation offered by the tenancy by the entirety (in some states) stems from the husband's exclusive right to possession during his life and the wife's exclusive right to survivorship interest on the husband's death. Further, the fact that neither spouse, acting alone, can transfer or encumber the property (subject it to a charge or liability) during their joint lives, prevents a creditor of either spouse from doing the same. It may, however, benefit a creditor to obtain "possession" of the property, even though a sale may not be possible.

A creditor of the *husband* may obtain a court judgment against him and may place a lien or attachment on the entireties property, as in the Gluskin case, above, but as a general rule, the property will not be ordered sold to satisfy the debt so long as the wife is alive. If the husband dies and his wife survives him, the lien of the husband's creditor is then ineffective (it is canceled on the husband's death) and the wife may take possession and control of the property free of the lien and free of the claim of her husband's creditors.

Although the property may not be sold, however, may the husband's interest be sold? The husband's interest in the entireties property includes his right to possession and rents during his life. In many cases, the husband's creditors have tried to take possession of the property and/or rents to satisfy the debt during the joint lives of husband and wife. Most of these cases (but not all) hold that the wife also has a right to possession and that the rights of the wife are unaffected by the judgment against the husband. However, if the husband survives the wife, then the creditors may reach and sell the *whole* property to satisfy the judgment against him.

The fact that the purchase price was not contributed equally by the husband and wife for the entireties property seems to have little effect on the courts' attitude toward this type of ownership. The common law concepts of possession, inalienability, and survivorship seem to be staunchly defended by the courts in many, but not all, of those states where tenancy by the entirety is still recognized. Perhaps the reason for the inconsistencies has to do with the so-called Married Women's Acts, and most recently, the Equal Rights Amendment. Because of these developments, many conflicting theories and a great deal of confusion has resulted with respect to a tenancy by the entirety. For example, in some jurisdictions, although it is agreed that the creditor of one spouse may not sell the property (since neither spouse may sell it without the consent of the other), it has been held that the creditor may be put into *possession* of the property with the spouse and to share the use and occupancy of the property.

Still other jurisdictions hold that the Married Women's Acts do not apply to the tenancy by the entirety. And the recent Equal Rights Amendment prohibiting, among other things, sex discrimination, promulgates principles that conflict with the common law concepts of the tenancy by the entirety. Those states that recognize both laws will have to enact some new ones. For example, Massachusetts, which has adopted the Equal Rights Amendment and which at the same time recognizes the tenancy by the entirety, is living in effect with two contradictory laws. In dealing with this dilemma the Massachusetts courts began to decide entirety cases in a way that drifted from the common law principles, giving the wife more rights, but the matter was really one for the legislature. Consequently, laws were enacted that specifically give the spouses *equal rights* to possession, rents, and profits on property held under a tenancy by the entirety. In addition, Massachusetts enacted a law that protects tenancy-by-the-entirety property from the reach of creditors of the other spouse, if the property is the couple's principal residence. This protection, of course, would not apply to a bank holding a mortgage on the property.

The problem now is that the new laws enacted to correct the old problems generally apply only to new tenancies—those created after the date of the new laws. Therefore, the old problems of the inequitable, discriminatory rights in favor of the husband still apply to old tenancies by the entirety!

What to do? For tenancies by the entireties created before these acts, it is probable that the common law concepts still apply. In any event, you should determine how the present state laws will affect your own tenancy by the entirety in case of lawsuit or death. Once you know your alternatives, you can make a decision whether to keep the tenancy or change it, since it may no longer provide the insulation it once offered.

Still another special exception applies when the federal Bankruptcy Code comes into play. If one of the spouses is involved in personal bankruptcy, then any property held by him or her as a tenant by the entirety may be *sold* by the trustee in bankruptcy, and part of the proceeds—relating to the bankrupt tenant's interest— applied to satisfy the creditors. If the property is sold, it is up to the other (nonbankrupt) spouse to claim his or her interest in the proceeds of the sale.

Whether or not your residence (if held under a tenancy by the entirety) can be sold out from under you if your spouse files personal bankruptcy will largely depend on the law of your particular state, but the Bankruptcy Code does give the Trustee in Bankruptcy the right to sell "all" the bankrupt person's property. Whether a special exemption may apply depends upon state law.

HOW CAN A TENANCY BY THE ENTIRETY BE TERMINATED?

As mentioned previously in this chapter, neither spouse, acting alone, may terminate the tenancy by a sale or other transfer of the property without the other spouse's consent. Of course, if *both* spouses agree to a transfer, the tenancy may be terminated. The transfer need not be to a third party. On a transfer of the property to either one of the spouses the tenancy would thereby be terminated. One way, then, to terminate the tenancy by the entirety is *by agreement* of the spouses. The others, we will see, are by death or divorce.

TERMINATION BY DIVORCE

As explained, the tenancy by the entirety requires the existence of the marital relationship. Therefore, a termination of the marital relationship such as through a legal decree of divorce will, in effect, terminate the tenancy by the entirety, since an essential element has been taken away. If terminated by reason of divorce, the tenancy by the entirety generally becomes a tenancy in common. The further effects of divorce in tenancy by the entirety are discussed in detail in Chapter 9.

TERMINATION BY DEATH

The marital relationship is, of course, terminated on the death of either spouse. This in turn will terminate the tenancy by the entirety, and the surviving spouse will be entitled to the whole of the property absolutely and free of claims of creditors of the deceased spouse. Occasionally, however, a problem can arise when the spouse who dies leaves the property (which he or she holds under a tenancy by the entirety) to someone else. This is similar to the problem discussed in Chapter 2 on joint property, when the joint property is left to someone other than the surviving joint owner. Because of the special nature of the tenancy by the entirety a slightly stronger argument may be made on behalf of the surviving tenant by the entirety as opposed to the surviving joint tenant, but the question must be asked—why create the problem and confusion in the first place?

Anyone who holds property as a tenant by the entirety should be careful not to dispose of the property in his or her will except on the condition that his or her spouse does not survive. For example, Bert, who is married to Bertha, could say in his will: "If my wife, Bertha, should predecease me, then I devise and bequeath the property now owned by myself and Bertha as tenants by the entirety to my cousin, Bruce." In this case, Bruce would inherit the property on Bert's death only if Bertha predeceased Bert, but if Bertha survived Bert, she would already have the property as surviving tenant.

SUMMARY

TENANCY BY THE ENTIRETY IS a special form of joint tenancy available only to husband and wife and only while they are married. During this period, neither spouse, acting alone, can terminate the tenancy by attempting to sell or transfer the property held under a tenancy by the entirety. This special form of ownership is created when property is transferred to husband and wife and can be terminated only by death, divorce, or by agreement of the parties. In some states, property held under a tenancy by the entirety may not be reachable by creditors of one spouse, but if both spouses are liable on a debt and the property has been pledged as security for the loan (such as a mortgage), the property is vulnerable to the creditor. Like all forms of co-tenancy, a tenancy by the entirety is based upon a combination of common law and laws of the individual states. Some states have abolished the tenancy by the entirety while others have enacted laws changing the common law characteristics of this form of ownership to reflect the "equal rights" of husband and wife. In any event, the changes and developments generally do not apply to the old tenancies, so the old laws may still apply to your tenancy by the entirety.

Since each state's laws vary, the acquisition or continuance of title to property under a tenancy by the entirety should not be made without reviewing the laws of your particular state.

5

RIGHTS AND RESPONSIBILITIES BETWEEN CO-TENANTS

ONCE WE HAVE A BASIC understanding of the different types of co-tenancies—joint tenancy, tenancy in common, and tenancy by the entirety—it is important that we understand the rights and responsibilities that exist between the co-tenants. With only a few exceptions, the relationships discussed here will apply to *all co-tenants,* whether joint tenants, tenants in common, or tenants by the entirety, since in each case there exists between the co-tenants a relationship of mutual trust and confidence with respect to the commonly held property. However, even though these rights and responsibilities technically exist with virtually all types of property, for practical purposes they are most apparent in those cases where there is a co-tenancy in real estate or *tangible* personal property. Examples of tangible personal property would be automobiles, furnishings, jewelry, and so forth, as opposed to *intangible* personal property such as securities or bank accounts.

1. DOES A CO-TENANT HAVE THE RIGHT TO USE AND OCCUPY THE PROPERTY AT HIS CONVENIENCE?

THE NATURE OF A CO-TENANCY itself suggests that each co-tenant owns an undivided interest in the whole property. Since the interest is undivided (not physically segregated), then possession need not be (although it may be) reduced to a particular portion of the property. In other words, possession, like the co-tenants' interest, may also be "undivided." This means that any co-tenant has a right to enter upon the common property and take possession of the *whole* of it. But this right is subject only to the *equal and simultaneous right* of all other co-tenants to do the same. Of course, it may be physically impossible for all of the co-tenants to occupy the same property at the same time, for example, a small vacation cottage, a car, or a piece of farm equipment or machinery. In such cases it is a good idea for the co-tenants to have an agreement as to the use and possession of the common property. They may (but need not) agree upon equal use. Whatever their agreement, it can always be changed if the co-tenants desire, but until it is, each co-tenant is bound by it. Therefore, if the use is not equal, it may be a good idea to provide that the agreement will last for, say, a year at a time.

If either co-tenant violates the agreement by retaining possession after the agreed period or share, he will be responsible to the other co-tenant for the period of over-use, possibly by way of a rental payment. If the parties cannot agree on a fair arrangement for use of the property, perhaps they should not be co-tenants. If this is the case, the co-tenancy may be terminated and the property divided, or the property may be sold and the proceeds divided. *Once the parties agree* on their respective use of the property, when a co-tenant is in proper possession (according to the agreement), *the other co-tenant may not question his right to possession.* Furthermore, when an individual co-tenant takes possession of the whole property, the law regards this as equivalent to possession by all co-tenants; therefore, a co-tenant's occupancy of the common premises cannot be attached by a stranger or trespasser questioning the right to possession.

While a co-tenant has use of the property, his use must be proper and reasonable under the circumstances. He cannot, for example, make changes to the propety without the consent of his co-tenants, nor can he put the property to a use that was not reasonably contemplated by the parties. If he does, he will be liable to his other co-tenants for any damages or other costs that result.

For example, if the parties are co-tenants in a passenger automobile, a co-tenant in possession would not be acting properly in using the car in an auto race, and he would be responsible to the other co-tenant if the car was damaged as a result of the improper use. While a co-tenant has possession, in addition to reasonable use, he is also required to take reasonable care of the property. If he does so in good faith, he will not be liable to the other co-tenants for losses to the property.

2. CAN A CO-TENANT EXCLUDE OTHER CO-TENANTS FROM POSSESSION?

Although any co-tenant has the right to use and enjoy the whole of the common property, it should be remembered that in the absence of an agreement, he has no right to *exclude* any other co-tenant from the common property. If he does so, the co-tenant who is wrongfully excluded may be entitled to damages or court relief, as, for example, in the case of Mr. Swift and Mr. Coker, two Georgia businessmen, who, in the 1880s, had businesses right next door to each another. Their businesses were separated only by a small alleyway. They each owned the respective lots on which their businesses were located, but the alleyway was held by the two of them as *tenants in common,* for their common use. Coker, who was in the meat business, decided that he could put the alleyway to good use in moving his beef. He proceeded to construct a wooden frame across the alleyway, and secured metal slides and hooks to the frame so that sides of beef could be moved from one end of the alley to the other for storage.

Swift requested that the structure be removed and Coker refused, stating that the alley was as much his as Swift's and that

Swift was not using it anyway. Swift sought legal recourse by asking the court to order Coker to remove the frame.

While it's true, the court stated, that one tenant in common has the right to use the whole property, he does not thereby have the right to *exclude* another co-tenant from the use thereof. By the erection of the frame and beef slides Coker in effect wrongfully excluded Swift from the use of the property. Neither party contemplated such a use of the property. If they had, the results might be different. However, each had a right to enjoy the use of the alleyway, and the fact that Swift was not using it at the time of Coker's construction made no difference. Coker was ordered by the court to remove the structure.

This concept of use and enjoyment has little practical application to certain types of property such as joint bank accounts or securities held in a co-tenancy. In the case of a bank account, for example, possession of the account book has little value for the tenants; it is rather the possession of the money by withdrawal that is important. Once this happens, however, there has been either a division of the common interests or an exclusion from possession as discussed above. (This is explored in detail in Chapter 7 on Joint Bank Accounts.) When securities are involved, once again possession is of little value, since the "enjoyment" generally stems from the payment of dividends or interest (or the sale of the securities), and this will be paid according to who the registered owners of the securities are rather than who has possession of the certificate. However, if it becomes important for one co-tenant to take possession of his or her share of the securities, this can be done by "partitioning" (dividing) the property, as discussed later in this chapter.

It seems, then, that the question of use and enjoyment is more pertinent to co-tenancies in real estate and tangible personal property, where use and possession are integral to the enjoyment of the property. For example, a co-tenancy in an automobile or a boat suggests that the one in possession of the property will have the actual use and enjoyment of the property. It may be possible for more than one co-tenant to use and enjoy such property simultaneously, but this would depend upon the cooperation and agreement of the co-tenants. If they disagree as to its use, they will either have to reach an agreement, dissolve their co-tenancy, or submit to some other legal resolution of the dispute, such as a payment by the co-tenant in use and possession to the co-tenant who has been denied his rights to use and possession.

3. IF A TENANT FORGOES HIS USE, CAN HE BE COMPENSATED FOR IT?

IT SHOULD BE NOTED THAT THE liability of one co-tenant to the other for exclusive use of the property will generally arise only if there is a positive refusal or denial of use to the nonpossession co-tenant. If the co-tenant who is not in possession or use of the property allows the other to use and enjoy the property without objection, no liabilities will arise. However, if there is an agreement or understanding between the co-tenants that the one in possession will compensate the other for the exclusive use of the property, then the co-tenant in possession will be required to do so, as in the case of the Roberts children. D.C. Roberts and A.S. Roberts inherited some land from their parents and held the land as tenants in common. A.S. Roberts (Alfred), without objection by his brother D.C. Roberts (Daniel), occupied and enjoyed the use of the land from 1933 to 1938, and also farmed the land, which was fairly productive. In 1939, Daniel brought legal action in a Texas court against Alfred, asking that Alfred be required to account to him for the exclusive use of the land for the five years in question.

The court noted that although the common law provides that a co-tenant need not account to another for the use of the property if the non-user offers no objection, this rule does not apply where there is an agreement between the tenants for some form of payment or accounting for such use. In this case, the following question was asked of Alfred during the trial: "And you were supposed to be paying rent on the property yourself that you used?" and Alfred answered: "Yes sir, I certainly do." Taking this to be evidence of their agreement, the court ordered Alfred to pay to Daniel a share of rent for the portion of the property in excess of the share to which he was entitled as a co-tenant, that is, one-half of the reasonable rent for the whole of the property, since he was an equal co-tenant.

If it were not for the disclosures and evidence offered in court, it may not have developed that Daniel was entitled to rent. As the court stated, the general rule is that the tenant in possession has a right to possession without accounting to the others unless there is an agreement to the contrary. Quite often the agreement is an oral one and difficult to reconstruct when it is the subject of a later dispute. In the Roberts' case, it ended up in the Supreme Court of Texas. This means that the parties suffered through years of litigation and expense before the dispute was resolved. Though it may not be foolproof, a written agreement between Alfred and Daniel may have avoided a good deal (if not all) of the costly litigation and dispute.

Once again, these issues of use and enjoyment arise more with respect to tangible personal property and real estate than with intangibles, such as joint bank accounts and securities. This does *not* mean, however, that the relationship and liabilities do not exist with such property. It merely means that more care should be exercised when tangibles and real estate are involved. In any event, if there is a special agreement between the co-tenants as to the use and possession of the property, it should be clearly stated in writing.

4. IF A CO-TENANT MAINTAINS THE PROPERTY OR INCURS EXPENSES FOR REPAIRS, IMPROVEMENTS, OR OTHER COSTS, IS HE ENTITLED TO REIMBURSEMENT?

AS STATED PREVIOUSLY, A co-tenant in possession of the commonly held property is responsible for its reasonable care and maintenance, and in the absence of an agreement to the contrary between the co-tenants, he is *not* entitled to compensation for services rendered in managing, operating, or caring for the common property. This is so even if he is responsible for leasing the property, collecting rents, or finding a buyer for the property. The reasoning is that the benefit falls upon him as well as upon the other co-tenant. Of course, if the co-tenants have an agreement that compensation *will* be paid for any of these services, such an agreement will take the case out of the application of the general rule. On the other hand, if the co-tenant in possession incurs reasonable out-of-pocket expenses in maintaining or operating the common property, each of the co-tenants is responsible for such expenses to the extent of his interest, and the co-tenant who paid these expenses will be entitled to contribution or reimbursement by the other co-tenants for their respective shares. If they do not pay they may jeopardize the value of their interests in the property, since the co-tenant who paid the expenses may be entitled to reimbursement, as discussed below.

5. REQUIREMENTS FOR REIMBURSEMENT

For the co-tenant to be entitled to contribution or reimbursement for expenses, certain requirements must be met. For one, it must appear that there was a common obligation or liability to make the payment. In other words, if it was a *personal* obligation of the paying co-tenant no reimbursement will be required. A common obligation is, for example, a lien on the property for taxes or for work done (such as improvements) or for a mortgage payment due. If the payment or obligation was enforceable against the commonly held property, this would generally be considered a common obligation of the co-tenants and payment of such an obligation by one co-tenant would entitle him to reimbursement from the others. For example, if Bruce and Bob own real estate as tenants in common and Bruce pays the $1,000 real estate tax bill, he will be entitled to reimbursement of $500 from Bob. On the other hand, if Bruce had work done on some property of his own, and in an effort to collect for the work done, the workman placed a "mechanic's lien" on the joint property held by Bruce and Bob, payment of the amount by Bruce to release the lien would not allow Bruce to receive any reimbursement from Bob, since the debt was personal to Bruce.

Another requirement for recovery of expenses is that the paying co-tenant must show that he paid more than his share of the common obligation. If the co-tenant had a one-half interest in the common property and paid one-half the expenses or obligation, no reimbursement would be allowed since he only paid that which was attributable to his own share.

Finally, it must appear that the payment conferred a benefit on all the co-tenants and that the payment was a compulsory rather than a voluntary one. This latter requirement may sometimes pose a problem to a co-tenant who voluntarily pays for repairs or maintenance to the common property. In most states, however, a co-tenant who has made repairs that are considered necessary to the preservation of the property may recover from his co-tenants even though they have not consented to the repairs. Usually, this right is strictly limited to repairs and would not cover improvements unless it could be shown they were necessary to protect the property.

In the case of *Holt v. Couch,* both repairs *and* improvements were involved and the court approved both. S.A. Holt and R.M. Couch were tenants in common of property located in Southern Pines, North Carolina. On the property was a building that contained a small store and boardinghouse. Because Holt was not a resident of North Carolina, he allowed Couch, who did live there, to remain in sole possession of the property to manage and care for it. Couch found that the building was unattractive and unprofitable as a store and boardinghouse so he made some changes, additions, and improvements, converting the building into a modern hotel, the Ozone Hotel. That was around 1893. Couch paid all expenses, insurance, taxes, and repairs, and collected the rents generated from the hotel. Holt never participated in (nor objected to) the management of the property.

In 1895 Holt brought action against Couch to recover one-half the rents from 1891 to 1895. Couch did not refuse to pay the rents but rather took the position that he should be allowed to offset the rents with the cost of improvements and expenses paid by him personally.

The court agreed with Couch. They found that the improvements made by Couch were "reasonable, necessary and advantageous to the property, and were neither authorized nor objected to by Holt." Couch was charged with $850 (one-half the determined rental for five years) and was allowed to offset this with one-half the total expenses, repairs, and improvement costs, which amounted to $954.50. Since this was in excess of Holt's right to rents, Holt was ordered to *pay Couch* the difference of $104.50 (in those days, a tidy sum).

It may be that Couch should have notified Holt of the intended improvements prior to making them. Also, he probably should have sent Holt some sort of report or account each year showing the income and expenses of the property. Apparently, he did neither, but the court nevertheless sided with him in the interest of fairness.

Improvements are often distinguished from repairs, and it is generally held that a co-tenant who has made improvements to the property without the consent or acquiescence of his co-tenants is not entitled to contribution from them. The results of cases, however, in which one co-tenant has made improvements are largely based on principles of equity as we saw in the Holt case. If it would be inequitable to prevent a co-tenant from recovering his costs of improvements, the court may allow recovery. For example, if a co-tenant went about improving property and the other co-tenants stood by, without objecting, permitting him to incur the costs, reimbursement would probably be allowed. On the other hand, a co-tenant will not be allowed to arbitrarily improve another "out of" his property by making costly improvements that another co-tenant could not afford.

Generally, even though reimbursement may not be required when the costs are incurred, in the interest of fairness the co-tenant who bears the costs of reasonable improvements will be allowed to take this into consideration when the property is sold or disposed of or when the property is divided and the co-tenants take their respective shares. In many cases, for example, a person, believing he was sole owner of property, made substantial improvements to it and then later discovered he had a co-tenant. In such cases, the courts have held the co-tenant who made the improvements in good faith was entitled to contribution by the other co-tenant.

6. IF A CO-TENANT RECEIVES RENTS OR PROFITS FOR THE USE OF THE PROPERTY, MUST HE SHARE IT WITH THE OTHER CO-TENANTS?

AS A GENERAL RULE, AND (once again) in the absence of a contrary *agreement* between the co-tenants, a co-tenant who receives rents or profits from the common property is accountable to the other co-tenants for their share of the rents or profits. This rule may not apply, however, if the co-tenant merely rents (or sells) his own undivided interest in the property. In that case, he need not account to his co-tenants, since the person to whom he rents or sells his share merely becomes a new co-tenant with the others (see Chapters 2 and 3). The rule of accountability also will not apply if profits were derived by the co-tenant (in possession) from his labor. For example, if a co-tenant raises crops on the premises and sells them at a profit, or if he uses the premises to practice a profession, so long as he is occupying the premises with the consent of the other co-tenants and has *no agreement* to pay rent or share profits, he need not account to them for profits from his own labor.

In most other cases, a co-tenant who receives rents or profits under an agreement that binds the other co-tenants, or in which the other co-tenants acquiesce, must account to the other co-tenants for their share of the profits, regardless of the nature of the rents or the use of the property, as illustrated in the case of Hazel Daniel. Hazel was the daughter of John and Hattie Daniel. On Hattie's death, Hazel inherited her mother's share of certain property that Hattie owned in a co-tenancy with her husband John. This left Hazel as a co-tenant in common with her father, John. John, who had remarried, sought to keep the property from his daughter, Hazel, and together with his new wife used and rented the property for several years. Since Hazel was deprived of any use or rentals of the property, she sued her father and stepmother, requesting that they be ordered to *account* to her for her share of the rents.

It turned out that the income from the property was derived from the rental of rooms to women who engaged in the practice of prostitution and who practiced their profession on Daniel's property. In this regard, John Daniel and his young new wife, Ella, brazenly pointed out that since the premises were being used for immoral purposes the court should not compel an accounting, because to do so would be in effect to legally recognize and enforce an illegal transaction.

Humor and irony aside, the court recognized the rule that a division of profits arising from an illegal or immoral transaction will generally not be enforced between the participants. However, in this case, Hazel was not a participant or a party in any sense to the immoral transaction and, the court stated, she should be entitled to recover for his wrongful use of her property. To do otherwise would be to punish the innocent and reward the guilty party.

Hazel was granted her accounting, and after testimony and reconstruction of the activities that went on at the premises she was awarded $24,500 for her share of the "rents" over the period in question. To this John and Ella strenuously objected, claiming that it was far too large and that no concrete proof was offered by Hazel as to amounts collected by John and Ella. (Apparently most of their customers paid in cash.) It was pointed out, however, that John and Ella kept no books or records of the amounts they collected, nor of the amounts they spent, nor of the identity of their customers, and, the court said, they are therefore not in a position to complain that Hazel's evidence was indirect and circumstantial. Unless they could produce more specific records of account, Hazel's evidence would be accepted, and it was.

7. IF A CO-TENANT MAINTAINS THE PROPERTY OR INCURS EXPENSES FOR REPAIRS, IMPROVEMENTS, OR OTHER COSTS, IS HE ENTITLED TO REIMBURSEMENT?

AS STATED PREVIOUSLY, A co-tenant in possession of the commonly held property is responsible for its reasonable care and maintenance, and in the absence of an agreement to the contrary between the co-tenants, he is not entitled to compensation for services rendered in managing, operating, or caring for the common property. The reasoning is that the benefit falls upon him as well as on the other co-tenant. Of course, if the co-tenants have an agreement that compensation will be paid for any of these services, such an agreement will take the case out of the application of the general rule. On the other hand, if the co-tenant in possession incurs reasonable out-of-pocket expenses in maintaining or operating the common property, each of the co-tenants is responsible for such expenses to the extent of their interests, and the co-tenant who paid these expenses will be entitled to contribution or reimbursement by the other co-tenants for their respective shares. If they do not pay, they may jeopardize their interests in the property.

8. CAN ONE CO-TENANT CONTRACT WITH ANOTHER FOR USE OR RENTAL OF THE PROPERTY?

WE HAVE SEEN IN (1) ABOVE that although each co-tenant has a simultaneous and equal right of possession of the commonly held property, it is sometimes agreed between the tenants that one or the other will have the sole use. Although it is quite possible for the co-tenants to agree to a "free" use of the property by either of them, it is just as possible for the parties to agree that the co-tenant using the property will be required to compensate the other for his share of the "use." In either event, if there is an agreement, it is important to clearly state that the use by one of the co-tenants will not affect the nature of the co-tenancy. Otherwise, it may be vulnerable to attachment, as it was in the case of Grace Adams and her friend Isabelle Yeats.

Grace Adams owned a house in Marshall County, Illinois, which she planned to use and enjoy as her own for the rest of her life. On Grace's death, she wanted the property to pass to her friend Isabelle Yeats. Grace decided that the best way to accomplish this was to make herself and Isabelle joint tenants in the property, so that if Grace died, Isabelle would own the property as a surviving joint tenant. With this in mind, Grace caused the property to be transferred to herself and Isabelle as joint tenants, with rights of survivorship. The problem was, however, that although Grace had now given Isabelle, as a co-tenant, certain rights of use and possession over the property, she (Grace) wanted the sole use and possession of the property during her life.

Isabelle agreed to this, and they entered into a written contract that stated that during Grace's lifetime Grace was entitled to sole use and possession of, as well as all rents from the property. In return, Grace agreed to keep the property insured and properly maintained, and to do other things "as if she were the sole and exclusive owner." It is also significant that the last sentence of their agreement read "This agreement shall not, however, in any manner affect the joint tenancy of said real estate nor the legal incidents accompanying same."

Grace died several years later. As the surviving joint tenant, Isabelle assumed ownership of the property on Grace's death. However, the executor of Grace's estate claimed that the contract between Grace and Isabelle severed the joint tenancy, since Isabelle gave up her possession and certain other rights. The Illinois Supreme Court disagreed and said that the *intent* of the parties was clear. They did not intend to sever the joint tenancy. Isabelle did not enter into the agreement to give up the one-half undivided interest in the lease that Grace had just given to her. She merely contracted as one joint tenant to allow another the use and enjoyment of the property. As the court put it, "Had Mrs. Yeats leased the entire estate to a stranger upon the terms written in the contract, for the life of such tenant, no one would contend that this would have severed the joint tenancy." In other words, the court said giving even a stranger the mere right to use the property would not have destroyed the co-tenancy, so why should a co-tenant's exclusive use destroy it?

Grace and Isabelle realized the necessity of making it clear that the joint tenancy was not to be destroyed by their agreement, which modified their respective rights. By stating that the joint tenancy was not to be affected, Isabelle was able to claim the property by her right of survivorship. Bob Brown was not as fortunate.

In 1907, a parcel of property in Brooklyn, New York, was conveyed to Robert V. Brown and Emillie Cotter as joint tenants. In 1931 Robert transferred by deed to Emillie "all my undivided one-half right, title and interest in and to the premises." When Emillie died a short while later, Robert declared that the property was now his on the basis that right of survivorship in the property remained in spite of his transfer to Emillie. He merely conveyed his undivided one-half interest and not his "survivorship" interest. The New York Surrogate's Court for Kings County did not agree with Robert's argument and stated that Robert had conveyed *all* his interest in the property to Emillie, including his right of survivorship. If Robert had merely intended to allow Emillie the right of possession during her lifetime, while reserving the right of survivorship, he should have clearly stated that in the instrument he delivered to Emillie. The property passed through Emillie's estate.

9. WHAT LEGAL REMEDIES AND RIGHTS DOES A CO-TENANT HAVE AGAINST ANOTHER FOR BREACH OF AGREEMENT OR IMPROPER CONDUCT?

ONCE THE RIGHTS OF THE co-tenants are established, either through special agreements they may have with each other or as a result of the basic rights and responsibilities created by their relationship as co-tenants, they are obliged to respect these rights. If a co-tenant acts otherwise, he is responsible to the "injured" co-tenant. Responsibility may be one thing, however, and restitution another. How does an aggrieved co-tenant enforce these rights? There are several legal remedies, each obtaining different results. The particular remedy selected by a co-tenant will depend upon the nature of the damages, the denied objective of the aggrieved co-tenant, and the nature of the property itself. The available remedies include an action for *partition of the property*; an action requesting an *accounting* from the other co-tenant; an action for *trespass*; an action for *ejectment to* remove a co-tenant from the property; and an action for *conversion,* where a co-tenant is required to pay for property converted to his own use. Each of these remedies will be examined in this chapter.

PARTITION—THE CO-TENANT'S RIGHT TO FORCE A DIVISION OF THE PROPERTY

A partition is a legal proceeding by which property held by co-tenants is ordered divided so that each co-tenant becomes the sole owner of his proportional share of the property and his rights as to the other portions are terminated. Once the partition of the property is made the co-tenancy is destroyed.

The co-tenants can agree among themselves to a *voluntary* partition if they decide they no longer want to be co-tenants. However, the situation may arise in which only one of the co-tenants for one reason or another becomes unhappy with the co-tenancy. There are no specific acts or damages or circumstances that must occur before a co-tenant may exercise his right to a partition or severance of the property.

At the request of a co-tenant, a court can order the commonly held property divided among the co-tenants either by a physical division of the property or by sale and a division of the proceeds. It need not be the result of a serious problem; a mere desire to divide the property is sufficient. In some cases, a partition may be ordered when it appears to the court that the parties should no longer be co-tenants on account of the relationship of one or the other to some third party.

Such was the case with James Givens and Grover Dunn. Mr. Givens and Mr. Dunn, two businessmen, bought a parcel of land in Georgia as tenants in common and erected improvements on it. They then rented the premises for $300 per month to Dunn Laboratories, Inc., a corporation controlled by Dunn. Under this agreement, each gentleman received $150 per month. Mr. Dunn was the president of Dunn Laboratories and Mr. Givens, who owned 35 percent of the company, held a lesser office. Subsequently, the men had a falling out and Mr. Dunn fired Mr. Givens from the corporation. Not to be outdone, Mr. Givens notified

Dunn Laboratories, Inc., that as to his undivided one-half interest in the premises, he was raising the rent from $150 to $250 per month. The ostensible result of Mr. Givens' demands would be that Dunn Laboratories would be paying more rent but the full increase would go to Mr. Givens. Dunn Laboratories refused to pay the rent increase. Mr. Givens then brought a suit requesting the civil court of Fulton County, Georgia, to order that Dunn Laboratories must either pay the rent increase or allow Givens to take possession of the land. The Civil Court refused to allow Mr. Givens to obtain the unilateral increase in rent or to allow him possession of the land. Mr. Givens appealed to a higher court. The Georgia Court of Appeals agreed with the lower court that Mr. Givens was not entitled to an increase in the rent or to possession.

The court in this case recognized that the two men were having serious difficulties managing the property together. It went on to suggest if they could not agree to a fair rent or to possession, a *partition* could be sought if these difficulties continued. "In a case such as this," the court said, "it is needful that one person control the property and that can easily be done by partition."

SHOULD THE PROPERTY BE DIVIDED OR SOLD?

AS BRIEFLY MENTIONED ABOVE, when a court orders a partition it can do so in two ways. It can order a sale of the property and a division of the sale proceeds in proportion to the shares of the co-tenants, or it can order a "partition in kind." The partition in kind calls for an actual *division of the property* into as many parcels or shares as there are co-tenants, so that each co-tenant will receive a share of the actual property in proportion to his interest. If, because of unique circumstances of the particular property, one co-tenant receives a piece of property more valuable than that of the other co-tenant, the court may require the co-tenant receiving the more valuable share to pay a sum of money to the other to make up the difference. If this is not practical, or unacceptable to the co-tenants, then the property will often be ordered sold.

An illustration of this is the case of the Burman and Hendrickson families. In that case six people were tenants in common in a quarter section of land in Clark County, South Dakota. The way in which these six became co-owners originated with one Henry Burman who died in 1904 without a will. Henry owned the piece of property in question and the law of the state determined the right of inheritance of his property as follows: one-third of the land went to his widow, Katie, and two-ninths went to each of his three children, Grace, Arthur, and Vernon. The widow, Katie, then married Karl Hendrickson and they had twin boys, Kenneth and Karroll. Katie died in 1944 and in her will left one-half of her share in the property to her husband Karl, and one-fourth each to the children of her second marriage, Kenneth and Karroll. (To the children of her first marriage she left five dollars each.)

The land was thus divided as follows: Grace, Arthur, and Vernon (the children of the first marriage) owned two-ninths each; Karl Hendrickson, the second husband, owned one-sixth, and Kenneth and Karroll, the children of the second marriage, owned one-twelfth each. (Note that the interests of tenants in common need not be equal.)

The two families had some difficulties accepting one another as co-tenants, and so the children of the first marriage sought to have the property partitioned through a court-ordered sale and division of the proceeds. They claimed that the land was so situated that it could not be partitioned in kind (physically divided and parceled out) among the various owners without favoring some and hurting others. They asked, therefore, that the land be *sold* as one tract and the *proceeds be divided* into each co-owner's proportionate share. The second husband and the children from the second marriage did not agree that a partition in kind would be unfair to some of the owners and asked the court to divide the land rather than order a sale. They specifically requested that they (Hendrickson and his children) be allotted, collectively, the southwest portion of the land. That portion had on it all the buildings and improvements plus a hog house. They asked that the other three owners of the two-thirds interest be given the rest of the land, which had no buildings because of a forty-acre slough (marsh).

The South Dakota Circuit Court agreed with the children of the first marriage and ordered the property sold. The others appealed. The Supreme Court of South Dakota agreed with the lower court and said that the land should be sold as one tract and the proceeds divided to each co-owner according to his share. The court noted that the land was owned by six people, the largest individual interest was two-ninths and the smallest was one-twelfth. Even if the land was divided into only four parts, because Karl, Kenneth, and Karroll wanted their portions collectively as one, the effect would be to depreciate the value of the remaining parcels and perhaps even the whole of the property, both as to its marketability and its use for agricultural purposes. The co-tenants would receive more if the land was sold as one tract and the proceeds divided than if any of the co-tenants sold only their smaller interests individually. The court then ordered the entire parcel sold, so that each co-tenant would receive his proportionate share of the proceeds.

(It should be noted that in this type of remedy, any co-tenant may attend the sales proceedings and purchase the property. The proceeds then paid in by the purchasing co-tenant would be divided as ordered by the court, just as if they were paid in by a third party.)

Although a co-tenant can generally obtain a partition of the property when requested, there is one major exception to this rule. Courts will refuse to order a partition of the property if it is held by a husband and wife as tenants by the entirety. The couple can agree to a partition, but without such an agreement the court will not order it.

As discussed in Chapter 4, the theory behind a tenancy by the entirety is that the husband and wife are one. Because of this fictional unity, neither party acting alone may sever the tenancy, and a court could not divide the property as though they were two separate people. Once the parties are divorced, however, the tenancy by the entirety is destroyed by operation of law, and the parties then hold the property as tenants in common. When this occurs the prohibition to severance present with the tenancy by the entirety is eliminated and the property may be partitioned on request of either of the co-tenants.

SUMMARY

WITH THE EXCEPTION OF A tenancy by the entirety, any co-tenant can cause a legal partition (a severance or division) of the common property whether or not he has a claim against another co-tenant. However, the request for partition of the property must be approached carefully since the division may be in cash (from a court-ordered sale) rather than a share of the actual property.

ACCOUNTING—WHEN MONEY WILL SOLVE
THE PROBLEM

A partitioning or court-ordered division of the commonly held property may not always produce the desired objective of an unhappy co-tenant. It may be that he wants to keep the property intact and perhaps even wants to maintain the co-tenancy, but feels that the other co-tenant acted improperly by withholding money or property that should have been equally distributed, or by using money or property for himself when it should have been divided. For example, say that co-tenants Fred and Bob agree to rent their property and Bob agrees to collect all the rents. When Fred later asks for his share, however, Bob simply refuses to pay or just says he "spent the money." What can Fred do? Must he partition the property? Not at all. He has a right to an "accounting" from Bob.

If a co-tenant refuses to voluntarily account, the other may request a court to order it. An accounting is a detailed report showing all income and corresponding expenses, and what is left (or what should be left) for the co-tenants to share. Once the court has approved the accounting it can order the co-tenants to do what is necessary to meet their obligations to one another. In the example above, Bob would be ordered to pay Fred his fair share of the rents collected by Bob. If Bob did not have the money to pay, Fred could take it out of Bob's share of future rents until paid.

The right to an account need not always apply to a recovery of money that was collected by a co-tenant; it may also apply when one co-tenant is prevented from using the property by another co-tenant. Even though we have pointed out earlier (Chapter 3) that each co-tenant individually has the right to possession of the whole of the property, this right is subject to the same right of possession by the other co-tenant. If a co-tenant uses the property *without objection by the others,* he is not obliged to reimburse them for his use unless there is an agreement to do so. If there is an objection to use, however, or if one co-tenant excludes the others, he is responsible to them.

Therefore, if the co-tenant in possession refuses to allow or prevents the others from taking possession when they have a right to do so, the aggrieved tenants have a right to an accounting from the wrongdoer. In this type of case the accounting would result in the wrongdoer paying the aggrieved co-tenants for the fair value of the *use* of the property during the period they were prevented from using it. It should be remembered, however, that when this happens, the parties are treated *as* co-tenants. That is, if there are two (equal) co-tenants and one wrongfully excludes the other, the excluded co-tenant could recover only *one-half* the fair rental of the property since this is all he would receive if the property were actually rented.

Several of the above points and problems are illustrated in the case of Fred and William Mauch of Oklahoma. Fred and his brother William had purchased a small farm, taking title as tenants in common. They agreed to an arrangement whereby William and his family would live on the farm at no charge but the two of them (Fred and William) would work the farm together and share the proceeds. Fred had his own home a short distance away where he lived with his wife, Ruby.

The agreement worked nicely for some time. Fred and William harvested wheat crops, planted fruit trees, and operated a chicken business on the property until Fred's death in 1963.

Since the property was owned under a tenancy in common, Fred's share passed through his probate estate (in this case to his wife, Ruby) and not to his surviving co-tenant, William, as illustrated in Chapter 3. In other words, Fred's one-half interest as a tenant in common is treated as if he owned that share of the property alone, in his own name. The person (or persons) who inherit this share would then become a tenant in common (in Fred's place) with his brother William. In fact, this is exactly what happened. Ruby became a tenant in common with William and William was not too happy about it, as he told Ruby's attorney in no uncertain terms.

William stated that he did not want to discuss Fred's interest with Ruby, and he was quoted as saying that Ruby "was not to come back out there" and he "didn't want to have her on the place!"

From these statements made by William the court determined that William had indeed "ousted" Ruby from the property without cause or agreement. Although Ruby could have entered into an agreement allowing William to stay on the land and work the farm, she was not bound to do so and she did not. Instead, on William's refusal to cooperate with her requests, she asked the court to order an accounting. The court awarded Ruby her account and ordered William to pay her one-half the reasonable rental value of the property from the time of Fred's death.

This situation more commonly arises when two or more persons purchase a multifamily residence and one of them wants to live there. Such an arrangement is workable but only where the understanding and provisions are clear. For example, say that Alex and Judy purchase a three-family home for investment and Judy decides to live in one of the apartments. As equal co-tenants they would each have a right to one-half the rents (after expenses). But if Judy lives there, the total rent will be reduced by the amount of rent that her apartment would generate. Therefore, to be fair the parties should do one of two things. Either Judy would actually pay in the fair rental of her apartment and net profits would then be shared (as if all the apartments were rented), or the amount of the fair rental for that apartment would be added (although not actually paid) to the total rents for purposes of computing the shares, and Alex's share plus any shortfall of expenses would be made up by Judy, up to the full amount of her "rent."

For example, say that the three apartments rent for $300, $400, and $500 per month and Judy lives in the $400 apartment. The total monthly expenses are $900. If the apartments were fully rented they would share ($300 + $400 + $500) less expenses ($900) for a net profit of $300, or $150 each.

If Judy actually pays the $400 rent, she would then receive back $150 at the end of the month. If she does not, then the income would be ($300 + $500) which is $100 *less* than the expenses. She would therefore have to pay the $100 expenses, and in addition she would pay to Alex $150 which is his share of the "profits."

Both approaches achieve exactly the same result, but actual payment of the rent and refunding of the "overage" seems less complicated and easier to administer. In any event, it is a form of accounting to the other co-tenant, and if the fair share is not paid or accounted for, it may be obtained through this legal proceeding.

In addition to recovering for rents or profits, the right to an accounting may be used when a co-tenant *damages* the commonly held property or is guilty of "waste," causing all the co-tenants to suffer a loss. In such a case, the guilty co-tenant would have to account to the others for the damage done. The case of John Henry Love is an example of this. John Henry and seven other parties owned some land in Autauga County, Alabama, as tenants in common. The land was covered with a valuable growth of marketable timber. Two of the co-tenants, Bessie Sharp and Alice Davis, entered into an agreement with a lumber company which operated a mill in the vicinity and transferred the timber rights on the land together with the rights to "build roads and cut underbrush" necessary to take out the timber. The lumber company proceeded to enter the land and remove practically all the valuable timber.

John Henry and the five other co-tenants asked the court to order Alice and Bessie to account for the damage to the property. In granting John Henry's request, the court observed the well-settled principle that co-tenants may compel an accounting by other co-tenants who have committed waste by "denuding the land" of growing timber without the consent of all the owners, and thereby depreciating the value of land.

Although the court could not replace the timber, it could order a fair division of the proceeds realized from the sale of the timber.

And it did just that. Alice and Bessie were ordered to account to all the other co-tenants and to pay them each a fair share of the money.

As effective a remedy as an order for accounting may be, it must be remembered that, like any right, it should not be abused. To drag a co-tenant into court every other month for an accounting without real cause can only result in needless expense and a waste of the court's time, which could backfire on the co-tenant who requests the accounting. Finally, the legal request for accounting need not be brought separately, as with other remedies. It may be brought in combination with one or more others, such as a request for partition and an accounting to the date of partition.

TRESPASS—WHEN YOU ENTER YOUR OWN PROPERTY WITHOUT PERMISSION

Some remedies that a co-tenant may have against another may not involve a recovery of profits or disposition of the property, but rather may be a sort of punitive action for damages done to a co-tenant, rather than to the property itself. The right of action for trespass is just such a remedy.

An action for trespass normally occurs when one person enters upon another's property without permission. When a trespass has occurred, the law *presumes* that a damage has been done "even if nothing more than the trampling of grass under foot." With a co-tenancy, it is hard to imagine a case of trespass since we have repeatedly stated that unless there is an agreement to the contrary, each co-tenant has an undivided interest in the *whole* of the property and each has a simultaneous *right of possession* of the *whole* of the property. A trespass, therefore, would seem quite unlikely.

However, it is the "unless there is an agreement to the contrary" exception that can give rise to the problem. It is clear that co-tenants can agree to give one or another the *exclusive* use of the commonly held property, with or without cost, without destroying the co-tenancy relationship. When this happens, however, the co-tenant who is given the right to exclusive use of the property by the others then has a right to that exclusive use and possession, and if his peaceful possession of that property is disturbed by another co-tenant he may *sue* the intruding co-tenant for trespass.

The case of *Hutchins* v. *Rounds* is a good illustration of this. Goliath Rounds was the sole owner of Glen Aubin Plantation, a 200-acre tract of land in Mississippi. When he died in 1923, Goliath left the land to his six children who became the new owners as tenants in common. The children agreed among themselves to divide the land into six parts, one for each of them to use and occupy so long as he or she wished. The division was not a legal division of the property but merely an *agreement* among them that each co-tenant would have the exclusive use of a particular part. They remained, therefore, tenants in common, each with an *undivided* one-sixth interest in the whole of the property, but under an oral agreement that each would have exclusive use and possession of a particular part.

One child, Dinah, married a Mr. Woods and they had a daughter, Julia. Dinah then divorced Mr. Woods and married Jesse Hutchins. Dinah died in 1943 and her one-sixth undivided interest descended to her new husband, Jesse, and her daughter, Julia, in equal parts. Jesse Hutchins then married Dinah Perry and the two lived in the house together. When Jesse died in 1946, his interest from his first wife's estate (one-half of one-sixth) descended to his second wife, Dinah Perry. Through this maze of transfers, then, Julia and her stepfather's second bride, Dinah Perry, were to share in Dinah Round's one-sixth undivided interest. Trouble was inevitable.

Julia returned to Mississippi from New Orleans in 1947 with her husband and three children. She demanded that Dinah permit her family to move into the house and have exclusive use of one room and common use of the kitchen. Dinah refused. Evidently Julia did not believe in resorting to the courts for her justice. She determined the do-it-yourself method was best and devised a plan to move into the home.

One day while Dinah was out, Julia and her family appeared with their household goods at the Hutchins' home. The securely locked door did not discourage them. They proceeded to break into the house by removing slats from a window. They then reached through the open window, forcibly removing a hasp from the locked door. Once inside the house they selected the room they wished to occupy and removed all of Dinah's furniture from that room. They also assumed common occupancy and use of the kitchen. When Dinah returned home she saw what had happened and had no intention of taking it sitting down. She had Julia's husband arrested, and while Julia was out, Dinah boarded up the door leading from Julia's room to the kitchen. Finally, Dinah asked the court to declare Julia a trespasser.

In deciding whether to grant Dinah's charge against Julia for *trespassing,* the court made these observations: all of the co-tenants had been in agreement that each was to occupy a portion of the property; that as to the one-sixth that Julia and Dinah were to share, Dinah had been in peaceful possession of it for several years by the consent of all the tenants in common, and if Julia did not agree with the arrangement she had a proper avenue to enforce her rights—the courts. The court went on to say that a tenant in common who occupies a particular part of the property *by agreement of his co-tenants* may maintain an action of trespass against any of them for the same acts that would constitute trespass on the part of a stranger.

What Dinah's actual damages were as a result of Julia's trespass is hard to tell and incidental to the issue, which is the right of a co-tenant to enjoy the property, even to the exclusion of other co-tenants, but *only* where the other co-tenants have agreed.

As a co-tenant with Dinah, Julia had the right to rescind the agreement to let Dinah have exclusive possession, so that she (Julia) would have an equal right of possession. However, she went about it the wrong way. Had she notified Dinah of her desire to change the agreement, she then could have brought an action for an accounting, causing Dinah to be responsible for rent. If possession was her desire, it would seem that such would be difficult if not impossible without an agreement with Dinah, since two families in a one-family home can be a problem. And if no resolution could be made, a partition of the one-sixth share could be ordered, which would most likely result in a sale and division of the proceeds. However, it would be legally possible (although perhaps impractical) for Julia to recover her right to possession through an action for *ejectment,* as discussed below.

EJECTMENT—WHEN YOU ARE PREVENTED
FROM ENJOYING YOUR SHARE

In the case of Julia and Dinah, discussed above, Julia went about her entry the wrong way. After she made her demand on Dinah to be let into the premises and was subsequently refused entrance, she probably would have been successful in bringing an action of "ejectment." If she were successful, the court would order that Dinah allow Julia to enter onto the land.

Ejectment is a remedy available when one co-owner of property has ousted or excluded another from the common estate or any part of it, without cause. The action allows the ousted co-tenant to bring an action to recover his undivided interest in the property. Although Julia decided to do it herself, Daniel McMahon sought the court's assistance. Daniel brought an action for ejectment against his brother and was successful in recovering his share of property from which he was wrongfully excluded.

Daniel's father, Benjamin McMahon, died in 1829 and was survived by his five children: Daniel, John, Benjamin, Sarah, and Margaret. He left to his children a tract of land in Pennsylvania which the children took as tenants in common. His son, Daniel, however, had gone west, no doubt seeking adventure on the new American frontier. Back home, the four remaining children decided to divide the premises so that each child would acquire his one-fifth portion. The problem, however, was what to do with Daniel's one-fifth share. John devised a plan to solve the problem. He told the others that he had made payments on some of Daniel's debts and said he would act as Daniel's agent. He requested that his and Daniel's part should be laid off together, and he (John) would hold the two-fifths for himself and Daniel. John went into possession of the two-fifths of the land as if it were one tract and on it he occupied a house, a barn, stable, garden, and wagon maker's shop.

All was going well, particularly for John, until Daniel returned from his western expedition sixteen years later. Daniel assented to the division of the land by his brothers and sisters, but was justifiably disturbed that John would not let him on the premises. John claimed he was exclusive owner of the land he was occupying, and he would not let Daniel live on "his" share.

Daniel brought a suit against John for ejectment from Daniel's undivided one-half of the land claimed by John. The Supreme Court of Pennsylvania held that the agreement among the brothers and sisters acted as a partition of the land occupied by Benjamin, Sarah, and Margaret. However, as to the two-fifths of the land occupied by John, John and Daniel remained as tenants in common. Because John had ousted Daniel by denying him his right to occupy the land, Daniel could bring suit of ejectment against John, and being successful, Daniel could then go on the land and claim his undivided one-half interest.

CONVERSION

Conversion is a remedy whereby an owner of property may recover the value of the property wrongfully taken by another who "converted" it to his own use. The general rule is that a co-tenant *cannot* maintain such an action against another co-tenant who has taken possession of the common property. The theory behind this general rule is that because each co-tenant is entitled to the whole, the one who has possession cannot be guilty of a conversion by possessing something to which he is already entitled. However, courts have realized that this would result in an injustice in certain instances. For example, the rule seems to have no reasonable application when the common property is readily divisible (such as a load of lumber or a barrel of oil or box of books) and one co-tenant takes more than his share. In such an instance, courts generally recognize that an action for conversion *will* lie when one co-tenant willfully destroys the property or sells it so that the other co-tenant is *denied* future enjoyment.

For example, Richard Delaney and Coryden Root were tenants in common of a crop of corn growing in the Springfield area of Massachusetts. In 1866, the two made an agreement that each would furnish one-half of the seed and manure necessary to grow the crop. Delaney was to do the hand labor and harvest the crop and Root was to cultivate it with his horse and cultivator. The resulting crop was then to be divided equally between them.

Root, however, grew to dislike the arrangement and when Delaney called upon him to cultivate the land, he refused. Delaney hoed the crop as well as he could without it being cultivated. At harvest time, Delaney cut the corn and put it into stacks. The night after Delaney had completed this, Root carried the corn away without Delaney's knowledge or consent. He then proceeded to feed the entire crop to his cattle, which they happily consumed. The Supreme Judicial Court of Massachusetts allowed Delaney to maintain an action for conversion against Root and recover one-half of the value of the crop.

In considering the availability to a co-tenant of the remedy of conversion, some courts have attempted to draw a distinction between an unauthorized sale of the property versus destruction of the property by a co-tenant. There seems to be general agreement that if a co-tenant willfully destroys the common property, an action for conversion will be available to the injured co-tenant. However, a few courts have said that if a co-tenant merely sells the property to a third person, then the other co-tenant cannot sue him for conversion. The injured or aggrieved co-tenant may either disaffirm the sale and become a co-tenant with the purchaser, or he may affirm the sale and bring an action against the seller for an accounting for his share of the proceeds.

SUMMARY

WHEN A CO-TENANT HAS SOME complaint, injury, or is just generally unhappy with the co-tenancy, he can usually rectify the situation through one or more legal remedies. The several remedies available to co-tenants for the wrongful or unauthorized acts of another co-tenant may be applied individually or some in combination with each other depending upon the injury or complaint and the desired solution or restitution. Selection of the particular remedy or remedies is usually not a matter for the lay person to decide but rather should be the result of a professional opinion. However, a general understanding of the various remedies and their respective uses and applications should help the lay person in dealing with co-tenancies as well as co-tenants, and the corresponding rights and responsibilities they have toward one another.

6

CREDITOR'S RIGHTS TO JOINTLY HELD PROPERTY

WHEN ONE PERSON IS LEGALLY indebted to another, the law provides various means for the creditor to collect his debt. Questions often arise, however, when the creditor tries to collect against property only partly owned by the debtor, such as with joint property or other forms of co-tenancy. Can the creditor of one joint tenant reach the whole property? Can he at least reach his debtor's share? Can he force a sale or a division? This chapter will deal with the rights of one co-tenant against the creditors of another, and with problems a creditor may encounter if he tries to reach property that his debtor owns in co-tenancy with another. In short, do you have to worry about the creditors of your co-tenant: can they reach your bank account? Or your home?

Whether a creditor will be able to reach such property depends primarily on three factors: whether the debtor (co-tenant) is alive or deceased at the time the creditor seeks to reach the property; whether the property is held in a joint tenancy, a tenancy in common, or a tenancy by the entirety; what the state law may be. These factors will largely determine whether the creditor can reach the property in satisfaction of his debt.

1. DURING THE LIFE OF THE CO-TENANTS

JOINT TENANCY

A creditor seeking to satisfy a debt owed to him may attach his debtor's interest in property held in a joint tenancy if the debtor/ joint tenant is alive at the time of the attachment. (An attachment is a legal securing of property to satisfy a debt.)

The general rule followed by the courts is that during the life of a joint tenant, that joint tenant's undivided interest *can* be reached by his creditors. The theory behind this is that each joint tenant is able to sell or transfer his interest during his life, thus severing the joint tenancy between himself and his co-tenants and creating a tenancy in common between his buyer and the other co-tenants. Since each joint tenant can sell or otherwise freely transfer his interest, his creditor should be able to reach that same interest to satisfy a debt owed by the joint tenant to the creditor. The effect of the creditor's attachment on the joint tenancy is similar to the effect of a sale of a joint tenant's interest. The joint tenancy between the debtor and his co-tenants is destroyed and the creditor becomes a tenant in common with the other co-tenants. The other co-tenants remain joint tenants among themselves.

The case of *Frederick* v. *Shorman* provides a good illustration of this result. In that case Hilda Bjornsen bought a piece of residential property in Cedar Rapids, Iowa, and had the deed state that she and her son, Robert, were joint tenants in the property with full rights of survivorship. Robert later married Yvonne and they had a daughter, Roberta. Robert and Yvonne were subsequently divorced and a judgment for child support was entered against Robert. When Robert failed to pay, Yvonne went to court and obtained an order that if Robert did not pay immediately, his property would be attached and sold to satisfy his obligations.

Hilda then brought an action in Lynn District Court in Iowa seeking to have the court declare that Yvonne could not attach the jointly held property. She argued that when she added Robert as a joint tenant she had only intended to create a *future* right of survivorship in her son and not a *present* interest that could be attached by his creditors. "I was unmarried at the time I purchased the property," she told the court, "and he was my only child, my only heir, so naturally I put the house in his name, only if something happened to me, he would get the house." (Sound familiar?)

Hilda also argued that she and Robert had agreed that Robert was to pay her one-half of the purchase price and maintenance on the property, but he never did. Since he never paid anything toward the property, he had no real interest in it and his creditors should not be able to touch it.

The district court agreed with Hilda's arguments and stated that Yvonne was restrained from proceeding with her attachment and levy on the property. Yvonne appealed to the Supreme Court of Iowa.

The Iowa Supreme Court *reversed* the lower court's decision. It agreed with Yvonne that Robert and Hilda did indeed hold the property as joint tenants because the deed on the property clearly reflected this intent. It reached this conclusion despite the fact that Robert never paid for any of the property's cost. Since Yvonne brought her action while Robert was still alive, she had the right, as Robert's judgment creditor, *to proceed with her sale* of Robert's one-half undivided interest in the property.

TENANCY IN COMMON

A creditor of a tenant in common may clearly attach the interest which his debtor owns in the tenancy in common. This is a well-settled principle in the law. It must be remembered, however, that the creditor stands in the shoes of his debtor, and therefore he can only take the interest which his debtor owned. In this event the creditor becomes a tenant in common with the other co-tenants.

In a Colorado case, C.V. James and his family were tenants in common in a parcel of land in El Paso County, Colorado. Mr. James owned a three-fourths interest and his wife and children owned the other one-fourth interest in the property (tenants in common needn't have equal shares).

In 1931, William J. Fallon won a judgment against Mr. James in the district court of Boulder County. An order for collection on the judgment was subsequently issued, and the sheriff of El Paso County was ordered to collect the money owed. The sheriff levied upon the land and put the land up for sale so that the proceeds could be given to Fallon and the judgment could be satisfied. Mr. Fallon himself purchased the property at the sheriff's sale, and he received the sheriff's deed. The sheriff's deed, however, appeared to convey *all* the interest in the land. It made no mention of the three-fourths interest of Mr. James. Mr. Fallon went into possession of the land assuming he was owner of the whole property.

It was not until *eighteen years later* that Mr. James's wife and children claimed their one-fourth share of the property. Mr. Fallon resisted but the El Paso County District Court agreed with the wife and children. Fallon appealed. The Supreme Court of Colorado also agreed with the wife and children and held that despite the fact that the sheriff's deed purported to convey *all* the interest in the land, the only interest the sheriff could levy upon was that of the debtor, C.V. James, and *not* upon the interest of the co-tenants. Only Mr. James's three-fourths interest could be reached by Fallon. Therefore, when Mr. Fallon bought the land, he stepped into the shoes of James, his debtor, and became a tenant in common in the land with Mr. James's wife and children. The wife and children were allowed to claim their interest in the land, even though so much time had passed.

TENANCY BY THE ENTIRETY

As we saw in Chapter 4, the tenancy by the entirety is based on the legal fiction that husband and wife are one, and that one is the husband. Even in those states where the rights of the spouses are considered equal under a tenancy by the entirety, neither spouse, acting alone, can sever such a tenancy, since it is still regarded as a tenancy by one. This fictional unity creates unique consequences for creditors who seek to attach the husband's or wife's interest (except in the case of a bankruptcy, as discussed later).

As a general rule, if the husband and wife are *jointly* liable on a debt, the property they hold as tenants by the entirety may be attached during their lifetime and sold for satisfaction of their debt. However, if only the husband or only the wife is individually liable on a debt, the creditor will encounter a problem if he tries to reach that property.

Except for those states where tenancy by the entirety has been abolished or modified, creditors of the *wife* may not attach the property and have it sold. Since the wife herself is not allowed to sell her interest in a tenancy by the entirety, her creditor could gain no greater rights and therefore will likewise not be allowed to sell it. In effect, the wife's interest in the property is insulated from the claims of her individual creditors during her lifetime.

Except in those states (such as Massachusetts) where special protection is given by law to a principal residence or other property held under a tenancy by the entirety, a creditor of the husband may place a lien or attachment on the property since the husband has the sole right to possession during his life. However, as a general rule, the property will not be sold to satisfy the husband's debt so long as the wife is alive. (For a more detailed discussion of creditor's rights in property held in a tenancy by the entirety, see Chapter 4.)

2. AFTER THE DEATH OF A CO-TENANT

JOINT TENANCY

As we have seen, one of the essential characteristics of the joint tenancy is the right of survivorship, so that the surviving tenant becomes owner of the *whole* of the property after his co-tenant dies. In other words, the law provides that the interest and ownership of a joint tenant ceases to exist on his death. One consequence of this is that creditors of a deceased co-tenant may not satisfy their debts from the common property. The theory behind this is that the property does not belong to the co-tenant's estate but instead becomes the sole property of the survivors. Therefore, the creditor cannot reach the property because there is "nothing" to reach.

The injustice that could result from this rule is demonstrated in the 1969 Mississippi case of the Weavers and the Masons. Albert Mason and his wife Lou owned a dairy farm in Newton County, Mississippi. Using his own funds, Albert established four joint bank accounts in the name of himself and his wife as joint tenants with the right of survivorship. The accounts totaled about $40,000.

Several years after the Masons opened these accounts, Jack and Eleanor Weaver, husband and wife, purchased some cattle and farming equipment from the Masons. Although it was thought that the two couples were quite friendly, a few weeks after the purchase Albert Mason shot and killed Jack Weaver, then turned the gun on himself and committed suicide. Eleanor Weaver was appointed the administratrix of Jack's estate and sued Albert Mason (through his estate) for the wrongful death of her husband, Jack. The jury entered a verdict of $25,000 against Albert Mason's estate.

The estate of Mason, however, was insolvent and therefore unable to pay the full $25,000 judgment, unless the joint bank accounts could be included as part of Mason's estate. Eleanor then brought an action as a creditor of Mason's estate seeking to reach the property in the joint accounts to satisfy her debt. She argued that the money in the accounts really belonged to Albert Mason, i.e., he did not establish a "true" joint tenancy, and therefore the money should be subject to the claims of Mason's creditors.

The Chancery Court of Newton County held that Eleanor had no right in the joint bank accounts because on Mason's death his wife became absolute owner of the funds. As of the moment of

Mason's death, his interest in the joint accounts terminated. The funds did not pass to Mason's estate and therefore were not reachable by his creditors. The Supreme Court of Mississippi agreed that Mason and his wife were "true" joint tenants in the accounts, and Weaver's widow was *not* entitled to satisfy her judgment for the wrongful death of Jack Weaver with the funds from the joint bank accounts. Eleanor got nothing.

Unfair as it may seem, Eleanor Weaver could not collect from Mason's estate, even though there was enough of Mason's money to pay the judgment the court had given Eleanor for the loss of her husband at the hand of Albert Mason. Certainly, Mason did not have this in mind when he created the joint accounts. No doubt he opened these accounts as arbitrarily as most people do, and merely as a matter of convenience, never dreaming the funds would be "protected" from his creditors at his death—but in fact the joint tenancy *did* provide such protection. Was it fair? Is "fairness" a concern? It may not have been fair to Eleanor, but what about Mrs. Mason?

In this case, there are no clear answers to these questions, but the examples should serve to point out the seriousness of joint ownership. Its creation is so deceivingly simple but with such far-reaching complications one may be tempted to place everything in joint names to avoid all claims of creditors on death. It's just not that easy. As will be seen, there are tax and legal implications, as well as exceptions to the rules.

For example, as to a creditor's inability to reach joint property on the death of a debtor/joint tenant, there are two recognized exceptions to this general rule: when the creation of the joint tenancy is deemed a "fraudulent conveyance," and when the jointly held funds are subject to the payment of federal or state taxes. A third exception would apply in those states that have specific laws regarding creditor's rights against joint property. South Dakota, for example, has a law that allows a creditor to sue a surviving joint tenant for the debts of a deceased joint tenant, and the creditor may reach the joint property to the extent of the deceased joint owner's contribution! And Washington seems to take the position that a joint tenancy shall not cause a creditor to lose his rights. But these states are definitely in the minority.

FRAUDULENT CONVEYANCE—A TRANSFER
TO AVOID CREDITORS

Most states have adopted the Uniform Fraudulent Conveyance Act (or similar act), which states that a party may not gratuitously transfer property to another (including a transfer into a co-tenancy) if his intent in doing so is to defraud his creditors. The uniform act says that such an intent is presumed if the transfer thereby renders the party insolvent. Some cases have held that if a party puts his property in a joint tenancy in order to defraud a creditor, then that creditor may reach the jointly held property on his debtor's death. For example, the New York Court of Appeals in 1967 decided that if mutual funds were placed in joint accounts to defraud a creditor, that creditor could reach the funds at the debtor's death. Here are the facts of that case.

In 1953 Leslie Granwill and his first wife Jeanette entered into a separation agreement which provided that he would pay $150 a month for the support of their son, Alan, while Alan was a minor. Also, Leslie promised that if he made any gift, set up any living trusts, or made any gratuitous transfer of property during his lifetime ("which was not supported by full and adequate consideration"), he would pay his son, Alan, one-half of the amount so transferred. Further, Alan was to receive one-half of the proceeds from certain life insurance policies. Leslie and Jeanette were divorced in 1954 and he subsequently married Monica.

Leslie faithfully made the child support payments and also gave Alan an extra $14,000 for his college education. However, he purchased mutual funds having a value of about $38,000, part of which he took in his own and Monica's names as joint tenants with the right of survivorship.

Leslie died in 1963, the child support payments stopped, and Monica succeeded to ownership of the mutual funds as surviving joint tenant. Leslie never paid Alan one-half of the value of the funds, nor did he make a suitable provision for Alan in his will as required by the separation agreement. Instead, he left his entire estate to Monica.

After payments of the funeral expenses and other debts, Leslie's estate contained about $20. Alan sought to hold Monica liable for one-half of the $38,000 in mutual funds.

The Surrogate Court of New York said Alan *could* receive one-half of the funds as a creditor of the estate because the transfer of the mutual fund shares to Monica was a fraud on his (Alan's) rights as a creditor. Monica appealed to the New York Appellate Division, a higher court, which *reversed* the lower court and said that Alan was not entitled to half of the funds because there was no actual intent to defraud. Alan then appealed to the Court of Appeals, New York's highest court.

The Court of Appeals said that if Leslie's transfer to his second wife left the estate insolvent, then it would be considered fraudulent without regard to Leslie's actual intent. As discussed in Chapter 2, with joint bank accounts each party has the right to dispose of one-half of the funds. The court said that although Monica was entitled to one-half of the funds in the account absolutely, as to her husband's one-half interest, she only had an expectancy that she would receive it if she survived Leslie. For example, Leslie could have withdrawn his half during his life. Therefore, although a transfer of interest to Monica was expected, it was not actually completed until Leslie's death. So if his estate was insolvent on Leslie's death, the gratuitous conveyance became fraud as to his creditors, and Alan, as a creditor, could have the conveyance set aside.

The court concluded that Alan could have a claim for a portion of the mutual funds because of the provisions of the separation agreement. However, one other issue had to be resolved before Alan was awarded the funds. That was whether the amounts previously given him by his father should be applied toward the amount his father owed him at death.

In any event, it was decided that Alan, as a creditor, was entitled to reach at least a portion of the jointly held funds since the transfer made by Leslie into joint names was "in defraud" of his creditors.

The second exception to the rule that a surviving joint tenant will take all the jointly held property free of claims from the deceased tenant's creditors, is that the common property is usually subject to *taxes* on the death of the co-tenant. To the extent that the jointly held property is subject to federal or state taxes, the surviving joint tenant (or tenant by the entirety) will still own the property but be *subject* to the payment of taxes.

In fact, a lien (a legal attachment) automatically attaches to all property that is subject to tax in the deceased's estate. If there is not enough money to pay the tax out of other property, the jointly held property may be sold to pay the tax. And if the other property is used to pay a disproportionate share of the taxes, the executor or administrator may usually recover from the surviving joint tenants their share of the taxes. (For a more detailed discussion of taxes and joint property see Chapter 10.)

3. BANKRUPTCY—SPECIAL RULES

A GENERAL CREDITOR MAY BE able to place himself "in the shoes" of the debtor/joint tenant, but a creditor under a bankruptcy proceeding may be able to go a little further. The federal Bankruptcy Code has established some special rules for co-tenancies when one of the co-tenants is declared bankrupt by a federal court.

When a person is the subject of bankruptcy proceedings, *all* his property is under the jurisdiction of the court and becomes the property of the "trustee" in bankruptcy. This will include his interest as a *joint tenant, tenant in common,* or *tenant by the entirety.* Under the Bankruptcy Code, the trustee in bankruptcy may *sell* the property of the bankrupt co-tenant under *any* of the various forms of co-tenancy and apply the proceeds of the share of the bankrupt co-tenant to satisfy the bankrupt co-tenant's debts. It is up to the nonbankrupt co-tenant to properly claim his share of the proceeds of the commonly held property *before* they are applied to satisfy the debts.

If a nonbankrupt co-tenant is the true "owner" of jointly held property in which the bankrupt is his co-tenant, he must prove to the court that none (or only a part) of the commonly held property should be subject to the bankruptcy proceedings. This could prove quite difficult and, even if successful, could result in considerable expense. For example, say that Ben creates a joint bank account with his son, Bruce. It is entirely Ben's money and he added his son as a co-tenant only as a matter of convenience. Later, Bruce files personal bankruptcy and, as the law requires, he lists the joint bank account (with his father) as an asset. Under the Bankruptcy Code Ben must prove to the court that the funds in the account were his before he can recover them. If instead of a bank account he purchased securities registered in joint names with his bankrupt son, he would be able to recover only one-half the value, since a completed gift would have taken place, and Bruce (or his creditors) would be entitled to one-half regardless of the fact that he made no contribution.

In some states, protection against a bankruptcy sale is offered for certain property (such as a principal residence) held under a tenancy by the entirety but this is the exception rather than the rule. It could be that in the absence of other protection under state law, if one spouse files personal bankruptcy, the home could be sold and the family kicked out. You should check the laws of your state to see if you are entitled to any special exemptions; otherwise, be sure to marry rich.

SUMMARY

IN MOST INSTANCES, THE creditor of a joint tenant may be able to stand in the shoes of his debtor/co-tenant and reach a share of the commonly held property, *provided* the debtor is alive at the time of the attachment. If the joint tenant is deceased, his interest in the property automatically belongs to the surviving joint tenant and the unsecured creditor has nothing to reach. If the creditor attaches the interest of a tenant in common, it does not matter whether the tenant is alive or not; his interest can be attached in either case. If a co-tenant goes bankrupt, the trustee in bankruptcy can sell the co-tenant's property, and it is up to the other co-tenant to prove the extent of his interest so that he can recover his share of the proceeds.

7

JOINT BANK ACCOUNTS—
THE POOR MAN'S WILL

INTRODUCTION

IN THE UNITED STATES, IF NOT elsewhere, joint bank accounts are second in popularity only to apple pie. That is, everyone has had or will have some at one time or another and most of us continue to enjoy them. Unfortunately (unlike apple pie), their popularity is generally unjustified and they are frequently the source of contests and expensive litigation. Actually, joint bank accounts do not follow all the rules of joint ownership. In many respects they are unique and in some cases are not considered joint property at all, as we shall see.

The joint bank account is often referred to as the "poor man's will," largely because it is so simple to create and the creator can enjoy the property during his lifetime, while feeling comfortable that the surviving joint tenant may take the balance in the account at his death. Such a result, however, may or may not take place. For example, the funds in the joint account are often originally deposited by the creator of the account and not by the other joint owner, without giving much thought to disposition of the funds on death. The account may have been set up merely as a convenience for the true owner of the funds, to allow the other joint owner to withdraw funds only in emergencies.

If a court finds that there was no intention that the noncontributing joint owner receive the whole account on the other's death, then it will not pass to him or her. Frequently, in fact, the survivorship interest in the bank account conflicts with provisions of the deceased joint owner's will. Very often this leads to bitter fights among family members. The Lowry case is a good example of this.

After her husband's death in 1962, Mrs. Lowry ably managed her own affairs for several years until her eyesight began to fail. When this happened, Fesington Lowry, the oldest of her five children, began to assist her. Until the time of her death, however, she remained alert and reasonably independent. During the time of her failing eyesight she opened two joint savings accounts in her name and the name of her son, Fesington. At the time of her death there totaled about $28,000 in these accounts. During the same period Mrs. Lowry made out her will in which she left her entire estate to her five children in equal shares. No mention was made of the joint accounts, since she apparently felt her will would take care of everything.

On her death her estate totaled about $50,000, exclusive of the joint accounts, and Fesington, who was named the executor of her estate, proceeded to distribute the estate (but *not* the joint accounts) equally among the five children (approximately $10,000 each), including himself. Fesington's brother and three sisters requested their share of the joint accounts, arguing that their mother's will obviously expressed her wish that all the children be treated equally. Fesington refused, whereupon the brother and sisters retained a lawyer and sued Fesington for what they felt their mother wanted them to have.

The action was initially brought in the Chancery Court, Knox County, Tennessee. The Chancellor found that the joint bank accounts were validly created and that Fesington was entitled to a survivorship interest in the accounts. His brother and sisters then appealed this decision to the Court of Appeals, and won (the Court of Appeals reversed the Chancery Court's decision). Undaunted,

Fesington then brought the matter before Tennessee's highest court, the Supreme Court of Tennessee.

The Supreme Court reviewed all the facts, examined the decisions of the two lower courts, heard the arguments of both sides, and reached its decision: in the absence of clear and convincing evidence of a contrary intent, a bank signature card that contains an agreement in clear and unambiguous language that a survivorship right is intended creates an enforceable joint tenancy with full rights of survivorship. The decision of the Court of Appeals was thereby reversed, and Fesington was entitled to the funds in the joint accounts.

What could Mrs. Lowry have done to provide some "clear and convincing" evidence to indicate to the court (after her death) exactly what her intent was with respect to the joint accounts? If we think about it, we can see that the only actual evidence was the account itself, governed by the contract printed on the bank signature card, something which, no doubt, Mrs. Lowry never read or thought about. If Mrs. Lowry wanted to clarify her intent she could have written a note to Fesington or to the other children, expressing her wishes that *all* her funds be distributed equally or that they pass to Fesington. Certainly, if the children positively knew that their mother wanted Fesington to have these funds, they probably would not have pursued it as they did.

It happens all the time—family fights, courts, lawyers, appeals, expenses—all over a question of intent. And the outcome is never certain. The Lowry case illustrated this by the different decisions of the different courts in the same state on the same issue. It can frequently come down to what a particular court thinks is fair under the circumstances. The Boots case is an example of how the courts attempt to apply the "flexibility" of the joint property laws to best satisfy the particular situation.

James Boots died at the age of forty on November 23, 1971, in the county of Outagamie, Wisconsin. He was the youngest of seven children, reportedly very shy, and quite self-conscious about his weight of 350 pounds, so much so that he rarely ventured out of the house and most of his personal affairs had to be carried out by someone else. For more than fourteen years prior to his death he lived with his sister, Catherine, who also helped him manage his personal affairs until 1957, when James's brother Henry took over.

It was shortly after Henry took over James's financial matters that James, his brother Henry, and Henry's wife Elizabeth went to the Kimberly Savings and Loan Association and opened a joint bank account in the names of "James Boots or Henry and Elizabeth Boots." Several years later, another joint account was opened at the Kimberly Credit Union under the names of James and Henry, jointly with rights of survivorship.

All the funds in these accounts belonged to James. Henry never used any of the funds for himself.

Everyone agreed that before James's death, the Boots family relationships were good. Both Catherine and her sister Theresa stated that they had always trusted their brother Henry, at least until James's death.

On the day after James's funeral, Henry and his brother Franklin had a discussion about the joint accounts. Franklin felt, as did his sisters, that James's money should be shared equally among them. According to Franklin, Henry replied, "Don't get huffy about it. We can settle it all and divide it up even." Henry denied saying this and later claimed full ownership of both joint savings accounts, which totaled about $15,000. After a great deal of bickering and accusation by Franklin that Henry had not acted "justly," Henry offered his brother and sisters $400 each to satisfy their complaints. They rejected this paltry gesture and finally, in September of 1972, they resorted to legal action against Henry, since he would not even tell them the amount of money in the accounts.

In considering whether Henry should have survivorship rights over the joint bank accounts, the Supreme Court of Wisconsin observed the presumption that a right of survivorship was intended when the account was created and that this presumption could be overcome only by "clear and convincing" evidence. What was clear and convincing about James's conduct?

The court felt *it was doubtful that James understood the meaning of the joint account,* pointing to his dependence upon others, such as Henry, for assistance in routine transactions. The use of the joint accounts, it said, was only as a matter of convenience and without the intent to give the funds to Henry. Apparently, the court felt all this was sufficiently clear and adequately convincing evidence that James did *not* intend to create a survivorship right in Henry, and the court ordered the funds distributed to the family as part of James's estate. Henry lost. But does that mean his brother and sisters won? It's anyone's guess how much it cost them in legal fees, lost work, and other expenses to take their case through the County Court and then the Supreme Court of Wisconsin. Was it all for their respective shares of the $15,000? Or were they so angry at Henry that they would have gone to any legal lengths to see the matter properly resolved?

And why were the results in this case different from the results in the Lowry case? Is it because the incidents took place in different states? Definitely not, since there are cases in each of these states that on similar fact patterns produced contrary results. Is it because there was no will? But Mrs. Lowry had a will. Are the results peculiar to these two states? Absolutely not.

There are literally thousands of cases involving joint bank accounts, and no state is unrepresented in this area. The cases are brought by parents against children, children against parents, and brother against sister, as we have seen.

From a purely legal standpoint, many states do not recognize joint bank accounts as *true* joint tenancies, and therefore no survivorship rights would exist. However, the overwhelming popularity of such accounts has caused many of those states to adopt laws recognizing their existence and establishing a *presumption* that the depositors *intended* to create a survivorship interest. In other words, if Ernie creates a joint bank account in the names of Ernie and Adele jointly, there may be a state law that says that unless shown otherwise it is *presumed* that Ernie wants Adele to get the balance of the account on Ernie's death. In states where there is no "statutory" presumption, the surviving joint owner must resort to other arguments to hold on to the funds.

This chapter will examine the creation and possible results of the various types of joint bank accounts, the presumptions, statutory and otherwise, that must be proved or overcome, and some ways to help avoid the serious problems that could arise.

1. THE RIGHT OF SURVIVORSHIP— HOPE SPRINGS ETERNAL

IN MANY, IF NOT IN MOST instances, the motive behind creation of the joint bank account is the hope that on the death of one of the parties, the survivor will be able to take the balance in the account without any trouble. This attitude stems from the public's general understanding of the joint tenancy and its attendant characteristics of survivorship. The joint bank account, however, is unique and may or may not be a "true" joint tenancy. Therefore, the question of the survivor having access to the account on the death of the other tenant remains just that—*a question.*

With a true joint tenancy, each joint owner has, as discussed in Chapter 2, an equal, undivided interest in the whole of the joint property as well as an equal right to possession and enjoyment of the whole. Clearly, such characteristics are not present with most joint bank accounts (with the possible exception of husband and wife accounts, as discussed later).

In the typical case, A opens an account by depositing his funds in the names of "A and B, as joint tenants." B is usually a "passive" joint owner with no real rights at all, until A's death or disability. That is, A retains control of the bankbook, receives all statements, makes deposits and withdrawals at his sole discretion, and has, in effect, full and exclusive control and enjoyment over the account. Under such circumstances, it would be quite difficult to argue that this arrangement constitutes a true joint tenancy. As will be seen, it may be that the depositor did not really intend or understand the results of a survivorship interest in this particular account.

The mere fact that the account is in the names of more than one person does not automatically make it a valid joint account with rights of survivorship. Similarly, the fact that words such as "joint owners" or "jointly" are not used makes little difference, nor does the alternative "A *or* B" versus "A *and* B."

In resisting a claim for the funds by some other party (including the deceased joint tenant's executor or administrator), the surviving joint owner must be able to show a *legal right* to the funds in the account. To do so, he may rely on one or more of the following arguments: a. that a survivorship interest was the *intention* of the deceased; b. that the survivorship interest was contractual—that is, a legal agreement among the depositors and the bank, as shown on the bank's signature card; c. that state law protects the survivorship right; d. that there was a "true" joint tenancy since the deceased joint owner made (or intended) a *gift* of the account to the survivor; or e. that their relationship as husband and wife protects their survivorship interests.

SURVIVORSHIP INTEREST *INTENDED* BY THE DEPOSITOR

Proving intent after the death of a surviving joint owner can be extremely difficult, since very often the opening of the account is done quite casually with little fanfare or discussion about the depositor's intention behind his act. It is common, for example, for a parent to open joint accounts with a child without ever discussing it with the child or anyone else. In such a case how do you prove intent? Answer: you probably can't.

Of course, there are varying degrees of proof. It could be just the actions of the deceased or possibly even the failure to act. Or it could be the discovery of an innocent conversation that took place between the deceased joint tenant and the teller at the bank, as in the New Mexico case involving the estate of Elmer Watkins.

In June 1930, Elmer Watkins opened an account at the Otero County State Bank in the name of "Mr. Elmer Watkins or Mrs. C.M. Watkins." Four years later Elmer died, and shortly after that Mrs. Watkins died. Since Mrs. Watkins survived her husband, the balance in the joint account belonged to her and would be distributed through her estate. However, the administrator of Elmer's estate did not agree and brought suit against the Otero County State Bank for the balance in the account.

The district court for Otero County determined that the funds belonged to Mrs. Watkins' estate, but the administrator of Elmer's estate appealed the decision to the New Mexico Supreme Court. (All this for an account of only $1,000!) The court said the fact that the account was in the name of "Mr. Elmer Watkins or Mrs. C.M. Watkins" was *NOT in itself sufficient to prove Elmer's intent* to create a survivorship interest in his wife; more evidence than this would be required. It was provided by two witnesses who appeared at the trial.

Mr. Spence, cashier for the bank, testified that he spoke with Elmer around the time Elmer opened the account. Spence said, "He seemed worried about money to take care of his wife if anything happened to him and wanted her to have the money in the bank . . . he didn't want his money involved in court . . . . It was then that I suggested to him to put their money in the name of himself *or* his wife, and have it understood with the bank that either could check on it during their life and in case of death it would be available to the other party."

The second witness, Mr. Lawson, who was an attorney for the bank, told the court that Elmer had expressed concern that the money would be "tied up in court" if he or his wife died. It was a few hours after talking with Lawson that Elmer opened the joint account.

The court found this evidence sufficient to show Elmer's intent to create a right of survivorship and denied the claim of the administrator of Elmer's estate.

It is unfortunate that so much time, trouble, and expense are repeatedly wasted on deciding these questions that could so easily be answered by the depositors themselves. In Elmer's case, for example, *a simple note* to his wife, to the bank, or even to the attorney clearly stating his intentions with respect to the bank account would have helped eliminate the problem.

SURVIVORSHIP INTEREST BY
CONTRACT WITH THE BANK

On the opening of a joint bank account the bank will invariably require each joint owner to sign a "signature" card which is kept with the bank's records for that account. The typical joint bank account signature card contains language to the effect that during the lives of the joint tenants each may freely withdraw any part or all of the balance in the account, and after the death of a tenant the survivor will be entitled to the full balance of the account. In either case, payment or allowance of any withdrawal relieves the bank of liability to the other tenant or to the estate of the other tenant. (In fact, this is one of the main reasons for the language on the signature card.)

The signing of the card by the joint tenants indicates an acceptance by them of the terms put forth by the bank. As to the question of how many of the joint account depositors actually read and understand the terms of the contract on the signature card (it is a contract among the joint tenants and the bank), that is another matter. It is often the question of understanding, or lack of it, that prevents the surviving joint tenant from receiving the balance of the account at death.

The trouble with the theory that survivorship is based on a contract is that the law of contracts must then be applied, and generally, to enforce a contract a person must show either that he furnished consideration or that it is a situation where consideration need not be shown. This can get sticky and legally involved. As a result, establishing a survivorship interest on the sole reliance of the contract on the signature card is generally a last resort. However, the signature card is definitely evidence of an intent to create a joint account, even though the depositors may not have intended to create or rely on a contract. But the question of *survivorship* intent still remains unanswered. To help eliminate this question, many states have enacted laws which *presume* a survivorship intention when a joint bank account is opened, as discussed below.

SURVIVORSHIP INTEREST BY PRESUMPTION OF STATE LAW

Because of the overwhelming popularity of the joint bank account and the equally overwhelming number of cases that have arisen questioning the disposition of the account on a joint tenant's death, most states have enacted laws dealing with joint bank accounts. The law that will govern is the law of the state in which the joint account is located and not necessarily where the owners live. The majority of these laws provide that a bank deposit in the names of two or more persons, payable to either or the survivor(s), shall be *evidence of an intent* to create a survivorship interest. Although details of the law vary from state to state, this type of law generally establishes a presumption of survivorship when a joint bank account is opened and a signature card signed by the joint tenants. Once such a presumption is established, clear and persuasive proof is required to overcome it (but it *may* be overcome!).

An illustration of this is the case of Boyd Wilson who, in 1944, deposited $4,000 with the Twentieth Street Bank in Campbell

County, West Virginia, in the joint names of himself and his wife Delania. In 1950 he added his sister's name, so that the account then read "Boyd or Delania Wilson or Prudence Lett." All three had signed the bank's signature card for the account.

Boyd died in the early 1950s and Delania died about a month later. As the sole surviving joint tenant, Prudence went to the bank to claim the balance of the account, which at the time was about $4,300. The bank, however, was concerned that the estate of either Boyd or Delania would also make a claim for the funds, and so refused to pay Prudence. Her only recourse was to sue the bank, which she did.

Although there was no evidence offered to show whether Boyd or Delania *intended* that Prudence have a survivorship interest, there was likewise no evidence offered to show that they did *not* have this intention. It so happened that West Virginia law provides that deposits to joint bank accounts may be paid to the survivor unless some contrary intent is shown. The Circuit Court of Campbell County held that Prudence was entitled to the funds. The case was then appealed to the Supreme Court of Appeals of West Virginia and that court also agreed that Prudence had a right to the funds. Since Boyd had followed the form (bank card) suggested by the law, and since it was not shown that he had a contrary intent, Prudence should get the funds, said the court.

It is ironic to note that the purpose of the law was to protect the *bank* from claims by the estate of a deceased joint tenant when the bank paid funds to a surviving joint tenant. And here, it was the *bank* that caused all the expense and delays, even though there was a law on the books that protected it in the event of payment.

Although the majority of the existing state laws regarding joint bank accounts primarily protect the bank, a large number of states have enacted laws designed to eliminate the question of intention as to property rights in the account. Some are *conclusive* in their presumption that the depositors intended the survivor to have the balance in the account, while others provide merely a *rebuttable* presumption. In other words, if someone can prove a contrary intent, the survivor will not get the funds.

The states that offer a conclusive presumption of ownership, such as Alabama and Vermont, are quite clear in their intent. It makes no difference that only one person deposited the funds, or that there was no delivery of the bankbook to the other, or that the noncontributing owner never had the ability to withdraw funds, *or* that there was *no intention* on the part of the depositor that the survivor receive the funds. Even in these states, however, if the deposit or the depositor was affected by "undue influence" (persuading a person to do something he would not otherwise do) or fraud, then there exists the possibility that the survivorship interest would be defeated. Furthermore, while the depositor is alive, he can always terminate the joint ownerhip by withdrawing the funds. And even though some statutes provide the conclusive presumption of joint tenancy, this does not mean that a creditor of the noncontributing tenant can reach the account, as indicated by many cases on this point. However, a creditor of the true owner may be successful in reaching funds in the account.

Despite the absolute nature of some of the state laws, questions and legal attacks on the joint bank accounts still arise. Even when there is a state law creating a presumption in favor of the survivor, the joint tenants should still make some clear expression of their intent, preferably in writing, rather than rely solely on this presumption.

SURVIVORSHIP BECAUSE THE DEPOSITOR INTENDED A GIFT OF THE ACCOUNT

It was previously observed that because of the unique features of the joint bank account, a true joint tenancy is extremely difficult to support. This is the primary reason for so many uncertainties over the survivorship interest. To the extent the survivor can show the deceased joint owner's *intent* to create a true joint tenancy, the question of survivorship will be materially reduced and possibly even eliminated. Intent can be proved by acts of the parties, or it can be presumed by state law, as discussed above, but this is risky to rely upon, since it is usually a rebuttable presumption, and even in those states where the presumption is "conclusive," the person claiming the funds can try to show fraud, undue influence, or mistake, or that the deceased was incompetent when he opened the joint account.

Another way to establish the intent of a depositor to create a survivorship interest (if not a present interest) is to show that the depositing joint tenant intended a *gift* of all or a share of the account either when the account was created or at some other time prior to his death.

To show a gift there must be more than just the creation of the account. There must also be an actual, constructive or symbolic *delivery* of an interest in the account to the donee (joint tenant) of the gift. This could take place in many different ways. It could be an outright gift of the certificate or bankbook itself to the donee, or a letter to the donee telling him that the depositor has deposited funds in an account for his benefit, or by allowing the donee to actually withdraw funds, or by some other act that clearly reflects an intention to transfer all or a share of the account to the donee joint tenant. It is very risky to assume that the creation of the account *itself* automatically establishes a gift, although in a few states such a presumption exists.

In the easiest and most direct "gift" case, A would open a joint bank account with B, then hand B the passbook, saying, "I have opened this account for you. Here is the passbook; use the money as you wish. If anything should happen to you before the funds are gone, they will come back to me since my name is on the account as a joint owner." Unfortunately, few cases are this clear, and the results will often lie with proof of the intent of the donor depositor. Still again, written expressions of intent or overt acts reflecting that intent can save time, money, and irritation for surviving joint tenants.

HUSBAND AND WIFE ACCOUNTS

Perhaps the two most common parties to joint bank accounts are husband and wife. The special relationship that exists between husband and wife itself gives rise to certain presumptions. One presumption is that each *intends* the other to have access to the funds during their lives and to receive the funds automatically on the death of the other; the second critical presumption is that a *present* gift of a share of the account is intended from the depositor to the nondepositor. All of this adds up to a presumption of a clear intent to confer rights of survivorship in both parties, and this rule generally applies whether the account reads "John *and* Mary," or "John *or* Mary."

In those states that recognize the tenancy by the entirety, it may be possible to have a bank account under such a tenancy, particularly when the funds deposited in the account are the proceeds from the sale of real estate that was held under a tenancy by the entirety. However, as a general rule, deposits by a husband or wife into a joint account for themselves are presumed to have the characteristics of a joint bank account as discussed above, rather than a tenancy by the entirety.

The existence of the presumption in favor of the surviving spouse should not in any way be cause for complacency about joint bank accounts between husbands and wives. Aside from the tax and other legal problems discussed elsewhere in this book, joint accounts—as should be clear by now—are quite vulnerable. Yes, the presumptions will help, but the idea is to avoid contests and litigation. If the husband has a joint bank account with his wife and at the same time has a will leaving the money in the account to his alma mater or to his children, you can be sure there's going to be trouble. It may be that his wife would be successful in protecting her survivorship rights, but why have the fight in the first place? If it's necessary or desirable to have a joint bank account, be sure that provisions of other documents do not conflict with the survivorship interest in the account.

2. CONVENIENCE ACCOUNTS— THE JOINT TENANCY THAT'S NOT A JOINT TENANCY

VERY OFTEN THE CREATOR OF A joint bank account opens the account merely to allow the other joint tenant easy access to the funds for the *convenience* of the creator. In these cases there is at least a tacit understanding that the funds are to be used for the creator of the account and they continue to belong to him. Such accounts are called "convenience" accounts and the nondepositing joint tenant acquires *no* rights to personal use of the funds, *nor any rights of survivorship* in the account.

Even though this principle is clear, there continues to be extensive litigation on this point and it generally stems from the inconsistent provisions for dispositions of the jointly held funds, as happened in the case of Fred Bamberger.

Bamberger owned a farm in South Dakota. He was a bachelor but had two nephews, James and David Barbour. James lived in the Chicago area and over the years visited his uncle several times. Daniel, on the other hand, lived in the East and never visited his uncle. Nevertheless, Bamberger had made a valid will in which he left all of his property equally to his two nephews, James and David, to "share and share alike."

Some time before his death in 1954, Bamberger added James's name to a bank account he had at the First Citizens National Bank of Watertown, so that the account read "Frederic Bamberger or James A. Barbour . . . As Joint Tenants with rights of survivorship and not as Tenants in Common." Bamberger made all the deposits to this account, which had a balance of over $37,000 on his death. James claimed the balance as surviving joint tenant. Bamberger's estate objected, claiming that the account was merely set up for Bamberger's *convenience* and he never intended James to receive the entire account on his death.

In reviewing the facts of the case, the court observed that the *intent* of Bamberger would be the controlling factor here, and that generally a presumption existed in favor of the surviving joint tenant, *unless* contrary evidence appeared. Part of the evidence offered by Bamberger's estate was a handwritten note from Bamberger which read: "James, if anything should happen to this body such as paralysis I think it best to get it [the body] down to Chicago in some place to be taken care of until the end comes just so as to be nearer the cemetery to save you trouble." In addition, a codicil (amendment to a will) signed by Bamberger after the opening of the account reaffirmed his bequest to the two nephews equally, making no mention of the account nor of any extra share to James. In fact, it appeared that James did not even know of the account.

Putting all these facts together led the South Dakota Supreme Court to conclude that Bamberger added James as a joint tenant purely for convenience, that Bamberger's note implied that James should use the account for Bamberger's hospital or medical expenses rather than for James himself, and that there was *no indication of any intent* that James have a survivorship interest in the account. Accordingly, the court ordered the funds paid to Bamberger's estate.

Convenience accounts also frequently arise between a parent and a child, when because of advanced age or illness it is convenient for the child to have access to funds in the account for payment of the parent's medical or hospital bills, living expenses, nursing home expenses, and so forth. Although the account may readily serve this purpose, it can certainly present problems if the child who is named joint tenant on the account is not the only child, particularly if the parent has made provisions in a will or trust that conflict with the disposition through the account. In these cases, a "letter of intent" should be written from the parent to the child indicating the intentions of the parent and the purpose of the account. Further, it would not hurt to have the child (or children) acknowledge their acceptance by signing the letter as well. This could help prevent costly litigation in the future.

3. OWNERSHIP OF FUNDS

IN THE MAJORITY OF JOINT bank accounts one party makes the initial deposit, and frequently the same party is often responsible for most or all of the subsequent deposits to the account. When there has been much activity in the account it is nearly impossible to trace the source of every deposit or the destination of every withdrawal to determine who "owns" the funds. Further, the question arises as to whether the depositing party intended ownership in the nondepositing party by adding his or her name to the account.

The general rule seems to be that unless evidence to the contrary is shown, the parties intended an equal ownership in the joint bank account. As previously discussed, some states establish this presumption by law, but even then contrary evidence may be produced to overcome the presumptions whether or not a state law exists; the burden is on the person attacking the joint ownership to show evidence that the deceased joint tenant did not intend the survivor to take the balance in the account.

In the case of Peter Fecteau, it was Peter's wife, Dorothy, who had the unpleasant task of proving that her husband Peter did not intend to have the balance in his joint bank account go to another woman. While he was alive, Peter added the name of June Larkin, with whom he was friendly, as a joint tenant to his bank account, and added the notation "either may withdraw—balance at death of either payable to survivor."

When Peter became seriously ill, his "friend" June went to the bank and withdrew several thousand dollars from the joint savings and checking accounts, then deposited the cash in her individual account. Peter subsequently died.

When Dorothy learned of the joint account with June she was understandably upset. On behalf of Peter's estate she sued June to recover funds she claimed belonged to Peter. The Court of Common Pleas of Cuyahoga County sided with June, but Dorothy appealed and the Court of Appeals found for Dorothy (the estate). Then June appealed and the Supreme Court of Ohio decided that the mere form of the account was not conclusive. It was a question of *what the parties intended,* and evidence might be offered to show Peter's intent on depositing the funds.

Because of legal technicalities the Fecteau case did not end there. Dorothy had to go back to the lower court to argue her case once again. It's hard to believe that a simple joint bank account would warrant all this litigation, or that there would be anything left in the account after paying the legal expenses.

4. CREDITOR'S RIGHTS

IN SOME CASES, THE ACCOUNT may be attacked while both joint tenants are alive, for instance, when a creditor of one of the joint tenants tries to reach the money in the account. Can he do so if the debtor is the *non*contributing co-tenant? In some states this is quite possible if the state has a law which provides that each tenant of a joint bank account has a "vested" interest in the account. A vested interest is one which legally belongs to a person—in effect an absolute ownership. Even where there is no state law, a court may hold that the creditor, once he is given a judgment against the joint tenant, may stand in the shoes of the joint tenant and, by virtue of the contract with the bank, be able to withdraw the funds in the account just as the joint tenant himself would be able to do.

For example, Benedict Track and his wife, Dorothy, opened an account at the Northwestern National Bank of Minneapolis. The card they signed stated that all funds deposited would be the property of the depositors jointly with right of survivorship in each, and that each party had complete and absolute authority over the account and that either could withdraw any part or all of the funds.

Benedict owed rent to an organization called Park Enterprises. Park sued Benedict and obtained a judgment against him. On the strength of the judgment, Park attached Benedict's bank account but Dorothy resisted, claiming that the joint account was not attachable for her husband's debts. Further, some of the funds in the account were contributed by her and therefore should not be reachable by Park. The lower court acknowledged that Dorothy had contributed and concluded that Dorothy and Benedict were equal owners. Nevertheless, Benedict's creditor could reach what was Benedict's and the court allowed Park to reach one-half the account. Benedict and Dorothy appealed. The Supreme Court of Minnesota saw things a little differently but still not in favor of the Tracks. The high court said that Park Enterprises not only could reach one-half the account, but was entitled to recover *all* of the funds in the account up to the full amount necessary to satisfy the judgment against Benedict. This reasoning was based on the contract covering the joint account, allowing *either* to withdraw the *full balance* without accounting to the other.

SUMMARY

OWNERSHIP OF THE FUNDS IN A joint bank account may or may not end up the way the parties intended, depending upon the circumstances of the attack and upon state law. Some states have laws establishing a presumption of a certain intent on the part of the joint tenants, while the laws of other states may establish conclusively that the parties intended a true joint tenancy. We have seen that in either case the account can be attacked either by successfully rebutting the presumption or, in the latter case, by showing, for example, that the original depositor was incompetent at the time he opened the account, or that for some other reason the law should not apply. In other words, ownership of funds in a joint bank account is somewhat unpredictable and to count on a certain result based on the existence of such an account is a calculated risk, at best.

5. WHAT HAPPENS TO THE MONEY WHEN THE ACCOUNT IS SUCCESSFULLY ATTACKED?

ALTHOUGH THERE ARE A number of ways of attacking the validity of a joint bank account, it does not necessarily follow that every account will be attacked. If there are no problems or people objecting to the account, then the funds would be freely withdrawable by either and would pass to the survivor on the death of a joint tenant.

If, however, the account were successfully attacked, what actually happens to the funds? The answer depends upon the nature of the attack, what the attacker is looking for, and in some cases, whether or not the deceased joint tenant had a will.

For example, in the case of Benedict Track above, Benedict's creditor was allowed to withdraw the funds. If Benedict had died before his creditor was able to obtain a court judgment, the creditor would have received nothing. In a sense it was not an attack against the joint account but rather an approval of it, since the creditor was "substituted" for Benedict as a joint tenant and exercised his rights of withdrawal.

An attack that produces a different result occurs when the estate of a deceased joint tenant claims the account was *not* a true joint tenancy, and therefore no survivorship interest exists. In this case *the funds would become part of the deceased's "probate" estate.*

The probate estate consists of all property that stood in the name of the decedent alone at the time of his death, and any other property or rights that must be transferred or exercised by the probate process. In general, joint property or property held in a trust is not subject to the probate process.

A joint account that has been successfully attacked, however, is no longer a joint account and would be treated as standing in the name of the deceased "joint" tenant alone. This would cause it to become a part of his probate estate. If the decedent died with a will, the funds would pass to the named executor and the executor would then distribute them according to the terms of the will. If there was no will, then the funds would pass to the "Administrator" of the estate (appointed by the probate court), who would then distribute the funds according to the laws of "intestacy" (when a person dies without a will). Where there is no will, the laws of the state of the decedent's domicile will apply, regardless of where the joint account was located.

There are considerable inconveniences in receiving the property through the probate process, such as possible additional executor's commission and legal fees and exposure of the funds to the claims of creditors, but there is little choice if a claim is in order against the joint account.

6. HOW TO REDUCE THE
JOINT BANK ACCOUNT PROBLEM

WHY ALL THIS CONFUSION, litigation, and expense over such a simple thing as a joint bank account? If the deceased joint owners had any idea of the trouble they were breeding they certainly would have taken steps to avoid this. But what steps could they have taken to avoid all this trouble?

For one thing, they could be sure that the disposition of their property under joint ownership is consistent with other expressions of intent or with any legal documents such as a will or a trust that are related to the disposition of that property. *In*consistency in expressions of intent will guarantee problems: for example, leaving your money in your will to one person when it is already in a joint bank account with another. As seen by the cases above, these facts are not at all unusual. In fact, they are somewhat typical of the arbitrary treatment most people give to joint bank accounts. If the surviving joint owner and the beneficiary under the will could work things out between them, there would be no problem. However, money has been known to cause people to act in strange ways and to do things they may not otherwise do, such as to take a position against their parents, or their children, or their brothers and sisters. If you had to decide some of these cases, how would you fairly resolve them?

As a practical matter, it is often taken out of the hands of the family. In many cases, the executor of the estate has an obligation to see that the question of the bequest versus the bank accounts is resolved since he has a legal duty to collect the "assets" of the estate and administer them according to the deceased's will and local law. The question raised is, are the funds held in the joint bank account an asset of the estate? As a representative of the estate, the executor would be required to bring the matter before the court for a decision (unless, as suggested, the parties could settle it among themselves). If the executor failed to do this, he could be *personally* liable to the estate or the beneficiaries. Therefore, he brings the matter to court. Naturally, the surviving joint owner would have to be represented since her or his interests would also be in jeopardy, and this is how we have the litigation, delay, and expense so often connected with such cases. If the deceased, however, provided in his will or elsewhere some form of written expression that his placing of the funds in joint names with the other joint tenant was with the intent that she receive the funds on his death, it is likely that the fights and expense may be avoided. Although this may appear superfluous since this is exactly what the joint account itself should provide, it would help eliminate any question if conflict later arises. The will, for example, could contain a provision such as:

DECLARATION OF INTENT. This is to acknowledge that I have or may have deposited funds in certain savings accounts in the joint names of myself and my daughter, Andrea. In the event my said daughter survives me, it is my considered purpose and intent that the contents of any such accounts shall, upon my death, become the sole and absolute property of my said daughter as surviving joint tenant, by operation of law, and that the funds therein are not to be considered a part of my probate estate, nor are they to be considered as being disposed of by this will.

This type of provision need not necessarily be in a will. A similar expression of intent might well be in a trust, in a letter from one joint owner to the other, in an agreement between the parties, or just in an informal written statement kept among one's important papers.

Of course, the language set forth above is for purposes of *illustration only* and should not be used without proper counsel. Every situation is different and each case should be diagnosed separately. Often many thousands of dollars are involved in the joint account or accounts in question, and a hypothetical passage from this or any other book should not be responsible for determining the financial fate of your family.

SUMMARY

THE JOINT BANK ACCOUNT CAN provide an inexpensive and convenient way of passing funds to other family members during life and after the death of the owner of the funds. That is, if no one objects. If there are some who are unhappy with the survivor taking the funds, it can also provide expensive delays, fees, and administrative costs as well as considerable inconvenience to family members.

The reason the joint bank account is such a popular subject of litigation is that the depositors take it for granted that there will be no problems. Where money is involved, however, problems have a way of coming up. Some states have enacted special laws in an attempt to avoid these problems by providing protection for the banks when the balance in a joint account is paid over to the survivor; other states have enacted even stronger laws that establish an immediate legal interest in the joint nondepositor as soon as the account is opened.

Obviously, the person attacking the account may have a greater burden in a state where the surviving joint tenant is protected by some specific law which establishes a presumption of intent of the parties, but this does not mean the account cannot be attacked. In those states where there are no such laws, the surviving joint tenant must show that he acquired his rights to the account under some principle of property law, such as a gift or contract, and must introduce evidence of intent to that effect.

It seems then that the single most important element in protecting the right of the survivor to the balance of the account is proof of the *intent* of the depositor. To help avoid future problems, it would be a good idea to record your intent in your will or trust, or by writing a short note to the nondepositing joint tenant (or tenants) plainly stating your wishes with respect to disposition of the balance in the account on your death or disability. It could very well save a good deal of time, trouble, and expense for everyone.

8

JOINT SAFE DEPOSIT BOXES—WHO OWNS THE CONTENTS?

LEGEND HAS IT THAT TO protect his great wealth the emperor of Annam (an early territory of India) had it all placed on a small island in the center of a lake filled with man-eating crocodiles. When he wanted to use any of the valuables, he would have the crocodiles killed, then later replaced to again guard his wealth. Today we use a safe deposit box.

Although it may not be as exciting as the emperor's arrangement, today's safe deposit box offers more safety and convenience but, unfortunately, some potential problems as well. With more than 30 million boxes in estimated use, one could hardly expect a trouble-free system.

Much of the trouble, or potential trouble, stems from the easy-to-do-it-yourself joint safe deposit box. Like the joint bank account, the ease of arrangement and lure of misunderstood benefits cause many of us to set one up without really thinking about the consequences or potential problems. Often, the primary reason we have a joint safe deposit box is to allow a spouse or close relative or trusted friend to have *access* to the box in the event of emergencies. Little thought is given to the disposition of the *contents*. It is just this question, however, that gives rise to fights and expenses after a death or disability.

Coins or cash or jewelry that is suddenly and unexplainably missing (just after the surviving joint tenant visited the box) from a joint safe deposit box after the death of the owner can make other family members wish they did have a lake filled with crocodiles—so they could throw the surviving joint tenant in. Sometimes it is so obvious that it seems just short of an outright theft. But is it? If the true owner didn't want the other tenant to have the property, would he have named him or her a joint tenant on the box? How do we know what his intentions were? Does the opening of a joint safe deposit box cause the *contents* of that box to be jointly held? This chapter will look at all these questions and some cases that illustrate the real problems with real people.

The difficulty, again as in joint bank accounts, is that there are almost as many different situations as there are joint safe deposit boxes. At least with joint bank accounts we know we are always dealing with money, and an identifiable amount at that. With the safe deposit box we could be dealing with anything from undetermined amounts of cash to unused airline tickets, from a Swiss bank account card to the key to another safe deposit box that no one else knows about. How can the family protect itself against an "unauthorized" joint renter who decides that the contents of the box are his?

One way is to document or prepare a general record of what you keep in the box and give a copy to your spouse (if you want him or her to know) or to a close relative or to your executor or attorney, and along with this, *make sure* they know your intentions (preferably in writing). But to understand the potential problems and why you should go to the trouble of writing these things down, you should learn a little about the basics of safe deposit rental.

1. BASICS

THE RENTAL OF A SAFE DEPOSIT box creates a special and unique relationship between the box renter and the bank. Basically, the bank agrees to rent space (in the form of the box) and to provide reasonable protection for access to that space. The bank need never know what is in the box and with the exception of a possible sale of the contents for nonpayment of box rent, the bank has no right to the contents.

The only persons who have a true right to the contents of the box are the *owners* of the contents. But here is where some confusion may arise. Don't confuse *owner of the contents* with *persons having access* to the box. For example, as employee of a brokerage house I may have ready access to their safe deposit box, but this certainly does not mean I *own* all the stocks and bonds contained in the box. The question is a little less clear when an individual simply names a spouse as joint renter, and we again ask, are the renters of the box automatically the owners of the contents, and if the box is jointly rented, does it follow that the contents are jointly owned?

First, you must understand the distinctions between renter and owner, renter and deputy, joint renter and deputy.

The *renter* of a safe deposit box is often the owner of what he might keep in the box, but it is not necessarily the case. John may have some gold coins that he gives to his brother, Bill, to place in Bill's safe deposit for safekeeping, or as in the illustration above, the renter may use the box to store property belonging to its customers, as in the case of a brokerage house.

Any box renter (including joint renters) may appoint a "deputy" on the rental contract. A deputy is very much like an agent and has full access to the box at any time until the original renter dies or revokes the deputy appointment. (In either event the bank must receive notice or revocation.)

If a box is rented in *joint* names, accessible to "either or the survivor," the rental contract merely addresses the use and accessibility of the box. The joint rental is an attempt to allow unrestricted access to the box after the death of one of the renters. In some states this works fine, but in others, the bank is required to "seal" the box on notice of a renter's death, even though the box is jointly rented. In such states access is allowed only if a government agent or tax officer is present to examine the contents.[1] In either case, the fact that either joint renter has access to the box has no legal bearing on the ownership of the contents. The subject matter of the rental agreement is basically the right to use an empty box. In the above example, if John gave Bill the coins for safekeeping and Bill placed them in a safe deposit box rented in the names of Bill and his wife jointly, would this have changed the nature of the transaction between John and Bill? Certainly not. And the majority of states follow this reasoning.

2. ILLUSTRATIONS

THE BIG PROBLEMS WITH JOINT safe deposit boxes come about when the joint renter is different from the person or persons who might receive the property were it not in the jointly held box. From a practical standpoint there would probably be no problem if, for example, Kenneth and his wife Maureen have a joint safe deposit box and Kenneth's will leaves everything to Maureen. On the other hand, if Kenneth's will leaves half to Maureen and half to his ex-wife Judy, it is likely that Judy and Maureen will have a problem. This is almost exactly what happened in the case of Dr. Ernest Wilson.

Ernest Wilson and his wife, Mary, had two joint safe deposit boxes at the First Trust and Savings Bank at Kankakee, Illinois. The joint rental cards stated "As joint tenants with the right of survivorship and not as tenants in common." Shortly after Dr. Wilson's death it was discovered that one of the boxes contained about $37,000 in cash (currency) and a handwritten note which read, "There is $37,000 in this box and it is a joint tenancy between my wife Mary Aldah Wilson, and myself. E.G. Wilson, M.D., 6–11–46."

Dr. Wilson also left a will leaving one-half of his property to his wife, Mary, and the other half equally to the two children of his *former* wife. As executrix of the estate, Mary did not include the cash in the probate inventory on the grounds that it was jointly held and therefore automatically passed to her without the need of probate. The two children objected and sued Mary, arguing that the joint rental of the box was not sufficient to cause a transfer of the cash to a joint tenancy between Mary and Ernest. The court agreed, pointing out that the rental agreement was merely a contract for accessibility to a box, and did not operate to legally transfer the property to joint names.

Mary argued that even if the rental contract was not sufficient, the note from her husband certainly established a joint tenancy. While in some states this might be true, it was unfortunately not so in Illinois, which adopted a law abolishing joint tenancies in personal property (cash is personal property) unless established by will or "other instrument" in writing. The brief note written by Ernest was not sufficient to qualify as an "other instrument," and therefore did not create a joint tenancy.

Mary was ordered to include the cash (and some bearer bonds) in the probate inventory, to be distributed in accordance with the terms of Ernest's will.

If you think about the rationale and logic behind this conclusion, it should not be a surprise. The surviving joint renter would have us conclude that all property in the jointly rented box became jointly owned. This application *might* lend itself to cash as in the Wilson case or perhaps jewelry or coins, but what about other types of property? If a person deposits registered shares of stock, recorded deeds to real estate, and several life insurance policies in the jointly held box, should we conclude that all this property is now automatically jointly held without the need for further transfers? And if one of the renters withdraws the stock or deeds or policies from the box, do they then become his sole property?

The answer is obvious. Neither logic nor basic legal principles would support such an outcome. Nevertheless, there are a few states that relax these rules a bit and, at least with respect to cash, have regarded the joint safe deposit box as similar to a joint bank account. The case of Eugene Adams is an illustration of this minority viewpoint.

In the fall of 1916 Eugene Adams, then about sixty years old, became acquainted with a girl named Jamie. They became quite close, and after a few months Jamie left her job at Eugene's request. Eugene gave Jamie a weekly cash allowance, and they took frequent trips together, traveling as husband and wife. In March 1918 they opened a joint safe deposit box at the Security Safe Deposit Company in Boston, as "joint tenants with rights of survivorship." Eugene placed $7,000 of "bearer" bonds in the box. (Bearer bonds are unregistered, and therefore cashable by the bearer, i.e., the person who has them.) Jamie was with Eugene at the time of the deposit and he told her they were intended as a gift to her. No other property was placed in the box.

On Eugene's death there was a dispute over the ownership of the bonds. The administratrix of Eugene's estate claimed the deposit of the bonds into the joint safe deposit box did not transfer them to Jamie, and Jamie, of course, claimed they were hers under the safe deposit contract and under the clear intention of the gift.

The courts held that the bonds belonged to Jamie. They found that the opening of the joint safe deposit box, the signing of the joint rental agreement, and the depositing of the bearer bonds in the box was the same as placing the bonds in joint names. The Massachusetts Supreme Judicial Court said "there is no difference in the governing principles of law between a gift of a deposit in a savings bank and a gift of securities deposited in a bank or trust company like that in the case at bar."

It is not clear if the result would have been the same had there been additional property in the box. In this case it was easy for the court to compare the box with a joint bank account. As with many such cases where the outcome is "discretionary" with the court, it could be that this result was the fairest given the fact that Jamie quit her job to be with Eugene. Nevertheless, the court had to have some grounds on which to make a finding. Here they found a completed gift on deposit in the box and there was enough evidence to support Eugene's intentions of a gift to Jamie.

If the party claiming the property can *prove* by evidence (other than the mere existence of the joint safe deposit box) that a gift did in fact occur, he will probably be allowed to take the property. In such cases, although placing the property in a joint safe deposit box may not in itself be sufficient to create a gift, it may carry some weight as evidence of the fact that the deceased intended the survivor to receive the property.

SUMMARY

JOINT SAFE DEPOSIT BOXES ARE an offspring of joint bank accounts, but perhaps a little more deceiving because they encourage a sense of complacency about disposition of the property contained in the box. The problem is it may or may not go to the surviving joint renter, depending upon the circumstances, the nature of the contents, and whether the nondepositor can show there was a gift or some other form of transfer of the property.

Further, too much emphasis is placed on whether the box is "sealed" or not at death. Those states that restrict access to a box on the death of a joint renter do so only to prevent property from going untaxed. They do not really care who gets the property once the tax is paid, except perhaps in those instances where the tax may be lower (or nothing) if the property passes to the surviving spouse, or to children. But they cannot judge this ahead of time so the boxes must be inspected. Whether your particular state seals a joint box on death should have little to do with the decision to have a joint box or not. The decision, if made, should be coordinated with the rest of your plans so that your property passes according to your choice with a minimum of taxes, expenses, and complications.

The majority of states clearly agree that the existence of the joint box does not by itself operate as a gift or completed transfer of the property within the box. If you must have all or some of the property in the box treated as jointly held property with the other joint renter, you should have a written agreement or statement to this effect with the other joint tenant listing the property and your mutual intentions with respect to it. If there is some property that is yours and other that is his or hers, this should be clearly identified or spelled out in the statement. In addition, you should register any property that should be registered (such as stocks or real estate), be sure that the disposition of the property in your safe deposit box does not conflict with disposition of the *same* property under your will, trust, or other agreement, and keep your fingers crossed that there will be no problems.

CHAPTER

9

JOINT TENANCY AND DIVORCE

INTRODUCTION—UNTYING THE TIE THAT BINDS

DIVORCE OFTEN CARRIES WITH it many painful but important issues that must be resolved between the parties. One of these issues is the division of property owned by each or both at the time of the divorce, and the way the property is held or divided can have a distinct effect on negotiations and on the legal and tax consequences of the settlement itself.

This chapter will examine separately the legal and tax effects of a divorce on property owned by husband and wife under a joint tenancy, a tenancy by the entirety, and a tenancy in common.

For purposes of this chapter, it is *very important* to remember that there are several legal distinctions between the joint tenancy and the tenancy by the entirety. Many couples make the hasty assumption that all property they own together is a joint tenancy, when in fact it is a tenancy by the entirety. This assumption usually stems from the fact that the property may be in both names and that there is, they have been advised, a right of survivorship. It is a common mistake to simply assume that this is a joint tenancy, when it may in fact be a tenancy by the entirety.

1. LEGAL CONSIDERATIONS

EFFECTS OF A DIVORCE ON A TENANCY
BY THE ENTIRETY

As pointed out in Chapter 4, the tenancy by the entirety is a special form of joint tenancy reserved only to husband and wife. Existence of this form of ownership is dependent on existence of the marital relationship. Since a formal decree of divorce terminates the marital relationship it correspondingly terminates a tenancy by the entirety between the spouses.

A decree of separation or a separation agreement between the spouses will not by itself affect a tenancy by the entirety since the couple is still legally married. A legal dissolution is required to affect the tenancy through divorce. But exactly what happens then? What are the parties' respective rights to the property after the marriage is dissolved by a court?

The answers to these questions are illustrated in the case of James and Laura Donegan, which is a reasonably typical case dealing with the effect of divorce on a tenancy by the entirety.

Laura and Jim were married in Alabama in 1864. In December 1870 they purchased some real estate in Madison County and took title as "James Donegan and Wife," which, the court held, created in them a valid tenancy by the entirety. Encountering some marital problems that could not be amicably resolved, Laura obtained a divorce from Jim in 1892. Laura then sought to have the property divided by the court so that she could have her share. Jim argued that they held the property as tenants by the entirety so that it could not be divided unless he agreed to do so, even though they were divorced.

In considering the matter, the Supreme Court of Alabama agreed that a tenancy by the entirety could not be severed by the act of one party, but also noted that that type of tenancy could exist only between husband and wife. Since Laura and Jim were no longer husband and wife they no longer could hold the property as tenants by the entirety. How then did they hold it? As this and numerous other courts have held, the divorced couple now owned the property as *tenants in common.* This means that each tenant's interest is now "severable"; that is, he or she has a right to have it divided without consent of the other, and further, there is no longer a right of survivorship.

In order for a tenant in common to exercise his or her right to divide the property, a petition (or legal request) must be filed with the court asking that the property be "partitioned" or divided. This "petition for partition" generally leads to a court-ordered sale of the property, because where real estate is involved it is often difficult and sometimes impossible to physically divide the property. Therefore the court will order the property sold and the proceeds divided.

Laura Donegan had a right to her share of the property and the court agreed. As a tenant in common she was allowed her right to a partition. The property was ordered sold and the proceeds were to be divided between Laura and Jim.

The petition for partition need not always result in a sale of the property. The parties could agree upon a price and one spouse could pay the other for his or her share. Nevertheless, the right to a partition belongs to all tenants in common and it makes no difference that they at one time may have been tenants by the entirety.

There have been cases, however, when husband and wife, by specific written agreement, have arranged to continue to hold property under the terms of a tenancy by the entirety, even *after* divorce. But this is certainly not the usual situation, and without such an *express agreement,* divorce will automatically terminate a tenancy by the entirety and leave the parties as equal tenants in common.

The conversion of title from a tenancy by the entirety to a tenancy in common does not require any further action by either of the parties—it occurs automatically as soon as the decree of divorce is final. If title to real estate reads "as tenants by the entirety," it is not necessary after a divorce to prepare a new deed showing the parties as tenants in common, but it may eliminate confusion if a copy of the divorce decree is recorded with the deed, to show that the parties are no longer tenants by the entirety, particularly if the divorce took place in another state.

Speaking of other states, the effect of divorce on the tenancy by the entirety will be as stated above even though the divorce occurs in one state and the property is situated in another, so long as the state in which the property is located recognizes the validity of the divorce in the other state.

As tenants in common, each party then has the right to partition the property (see Chapter 5), whether or not the other party gives his or her consent. A partition is either an actual division of the property or a sale and division of the proceeds. Because of the nature of the tenancy by the entirety, courts generally hold that divorce leaves the parties as *equal* tenants in common, so any subsequent partition would result in an equal division of the property or sale proceeds, regardless of the original contributions of the respective spouses, unless, of course, they agreed to a different division.

In addition to gaining the right to partition, each party *loses* the right of survivorship in the property which was formerly a tenancy by the entirety. A tenant in common has no right to take the share of a deceased co-tenant, and therefore each co-tenant's share passes through his estate. This means the share of ex-husband or ex-wife would pass to his or her respective heirs and not to the surviving ex-spouse.

Those general rules regarding the effect of divorce on a tenancy by the entirety are the law in most states but there is, of course, a so-called minority view, which holds that divorce by itself does not affect the tenancy by the entirety. Even in these states, however, the tenancy does not necessarily remain exactly the same as it was prior to the divorce. Because of the rapidly changing laws and attitudes toward legal/marital property rights, the laws in your state should be examined before relying upon the general rule.

EFFECTS OF DIVORCE ON A JOINT TENANCY

Because the existence of a joint tenancy does not depend upon the marital relationship of the joint tenants (as it does with a tenancy by the entirety), a termination of the marriage by divorce has, with rare exception, no effect on a joint tenancy between husband and wife. A very few states have laws which convert a joint tenancy into a tenancy in common upon divorce, but the overwhelming majority hold that divorce has no effect on a joint tenancy.

After the divorce the parties would continue as joint tenants unless the joint tenancy was modified or terminated by some other acts or agreements.

For example, it is possible for the parties to agree upon a termination of the joint tenancy and to have this agreement made a part of the divorce decree. In this case, it is not the divorce that affects the joint tenancy but the parties themselves by their agreement.

It may also happen that the *acts* of the parties subsequent to the divorce operate as a conversion of the joint tenancy into a tenancy in common. This occurred in the case of William and Juanita Ellis who owned a two-family home in Kansas as joint tenants. When they agreed to (and were granted) a divorce, they also agreed to equally divide the ownership of the house between them. In addition, the agreement gave Juanita the right to purchase William's one-half share for one-half the appraised value. Shortly thereafter, they entered into another agreement to sell the property and divide the cash proceeds. Up to the time of sale, each occupied and maintained one-half the house, and later each rented his and her side of the house. Title *remained* in joint names.

Before the house was sold, William died. His will left the property to his two daughters, but Juanita claimed it all was hers because of the joint tenancy and she was the surviving joint tenant.

The Supreme Court of Kansas held that the joint tenancy was terminated and converted into a tenancy in common *by the acts of the parties*. The individual agreements and subsequent conduct of William and Juanita with respect to the property clearly indicated they intended to sever their interests and not remain as joint tenants. Consequently, one-half the property belonged to William's two daughters.

Therefore, where there is jointly held property and a divorce takes place, the parties should agree upon a division of the property and the agreement should be in writing (perhaps as part of the divorce-settlement agreement) to eliminate any questions or problems in the event of death or disability of either party before the property is divided or sold.

EFFECTS OF DIVORCE ON A TENANCY IN COMMON

Property held by husband and wife under a tenancy in common is usually not affected by a divorce. Neither the existence of the marital relationship nor the dissolution of it has any bearing on their ownership or shares as tenants in common. As discussed in Chapter 3, each tenant in common can freely transfer his share either during life or through his estate at death, and so except for the fact that the property is commonly held, it is tantamount to outright ownership of the share.

Of course, the parties could agree that one or the other's share would be given up as a part of the divorce settlement, but once again this is merely a matter of individual negotiation and agreement and is not on account of the legal effect of a divorce.

SUMMARY

GENERALLY, THE ONLY FORM OF co-tenancy that is legally affected by a divorce without the necessity of an agreement between the parties is the tenancy by the entirety. Where this form of ownership is involved, those states that recognize the tenancy by the entirety generally hold that divorce converts the tenancy by the entirety into a tenancy in common.

In and of itself, a divorce does not affect a joint tenancy or a tenancy in common. Unless the parties agree or indicate otherwise, these two forms of co-tenancy remain the same after the divorce. But if the parties do enter into an agreement to sever the joint tenancy or tenancy in common upon divorce, then the divorce will be the triggering factor in bringing about the severance in accordance with the parties' agreement.

2. TAX CONSIDERATIONS IN DIVORCE

IT HAS BEEN SAID THAT THE Internal Revenue Service is often the third party in a divorce action as a result of the unforeseen tax consequences of property settlements between the spouses. What follows, although merely an overview of the general tax problems involved, may help avoid some of these tax traps, at least where commonly owned property is involved.

More often than not, the property subject to settlement is owned by the spouses jointly or under a tenancy by the entirety. There are special tax rules relating to division of such property on divorce and many of these rules are frequently overlooked.

A. THE GENERAL RULE—UNEXPECTED GAINS AND NONDEDUCTIBLE LOSSES

The general tax rule for divorce settlements, which was established by the United States Supreme Court years ago, still generates tax surprises. It is known as the Davis rule, named after the ex-husband who was sued *by the IRS* for taxes due as a result of the property settlement in a divorce. The rule is that *a transfer of property under a divorce settlement is a (potentially) taxable event to the spouse making the Transfer.* The reason it can produce a tax is that the transferor spouse is treated as if he made a *sale* of the property at the fair value at the time of the transfer.

In the Davis case, for example, as a part of the divorce settlement, Tom Davis agreed to give his ex-wife about $82,000 worth of stock for which he paid about $75,000. The difference of $7,000, the IRS said, was a taxable gain to Mr. Davis, even though there was no actual sale of the stock. The United States Supreme Court agreed. Davis had to pay a tax on the gain, and that has been the law since.

Since the law treats a transfer of appreciated property in a divorce settlement as a taxable event, it would seem that if the property had gone *down* in value, the transferor spouse would be entitled to a deductible loss. Well, he would be, provided it is the type of property that, if actually sold, would have produced a deductible loss.

For example, the sale of your principal residence at a gain is taxable (unless you defer the gain as allowed by the tax law), while the sale of your residence at a loss is *not* deductible. On the other hand, if it is stock or other securities, these should present no problem since a sale at a loss would produce a deductible loss.

With respect to gains and losses on different types of property that may be the subject of a divorce settlement, the laws can become quite involved and experts should always be consulted. For example, dividing business property that has been depreciated can produce serious tax problems for the transferor spouse. Further, the timing of the transfer can be critical in that in some cases it may be more advisable to make the actual transfer after the divorce when the parties are "unrelated" rather than before, when they are "related" for tax purposes, because, for example, certain losses between related parties are ignored for tax purposes and so the entire deduction could be lost just on account of poor timing.

As a logical result of taxing the transferor spouse on any gain recognized to him when he transfers appreciated property as a part of the divorce settlement, the transferee spouse (the one who receives the property—more often the wife) enjoys a "stepped-up" cost basis in the property. This means that for tax purposes on later sale, she is treated as if she paid fair value for the property at the time of settlement—the same value at which her husband, the transferor spouse, is taxed.

For example, in the Davis case, Tom Davis transferred stocks *worth* $82,000 to his wife but he had paid only $75,000 for them, so he was taxed on the $7,000 gain. The ex-Mrs. Davis, on the other hand, is given a "cost" of $82,000 for the newly acquired stocks, and if she turned around and sold them at that price, she would have *no* taxable gain.

Although application of this general rule to gains and losses may appear straightforward, it should be clear that it can likewise be complicated and confusing and can produce strange results and even exceptions when combined with other tax laws. One such exception applies where commonly owned property is involved.

B. EQUAL DIVISION OF COMMONLY OWNED PROPERTY—EXCEPTIONS TO THE GENERAL RULE

When there is an equal division of commonly owned property between the spouse co-owners, *no* gain or loss will be recognized to either of the spouses. For example, say the only property involved is a home held under a tenancy by the entirety and worth $80,000, plus securities jointly held and also worth $80,000. If the wife takes the home and the husband takes all the securities, there will be no gain as a result of the divorce settlement, since there was an equal division of the commonly held property. The same result would apply if they took title to *both* items as tenants in common, since this would also amount to an equal division between them (i.e., each would own half the house and half the stocks).

For purposes of this rule, the IRS considers "commonly owned" property to include property held under a joint tenancy, tenancy by the entirety, tenancy in common, and community property.

Remember that in the above example even though there is no gain as a result of the divorce settlement, either spouse might have a taxable gain (or loss) on a later sale of the property.

1. What Is an Equal Division?

In applying the general rule of nonrecognition of gain where there is an *equal division* of the commonly held property, problems can arise in determining what is an equal division. The IRS has indicated that it does not have to be "down to the penny," but correspondingly, large amounts of cash may not be applied to make up the difference. For example, a difference of $500 in a division of nearly $300,000 worth of commonly owned property was held by the IRS to be negligible and it was treated as an equal division. On the other hand, say there is $80,000 of jointly held property and $40,000 in cash owned by the husband. In a settlement, the husband agrees to keep the $40,000 in cash plus $20,000 worth of the joint property. Although it would be an "equal" division of all the property ($60,000 each), the husband would be *taxed* on $20,000 (that is, as if he *sold* this amount of the jointly held property) since this was the additional amount of the joint property he could have received but instead gave it to his wife as part of the property settlement. Looking at it another way, his wife was entitled only to one-half the joint property, or $40,000. Instead, she received more than one-half (she received

$60,000), so the husband is treated as exchanging $20,000 worth of the property in return for the wife's relinquishment of her marital rights. Therefore, the husband has received a *value* for this, and he will be taxed on it accordingly, under the Davis rule. Of course, if he paid more than $20,000 for the $20,000 of property he transferred to his wife, he may have a deductible loss.

To be equal and qualify as a nontaxable settlement, the division need not divide each and every asset individually, although if possible, this would be the clearest case. The division may be either on an asset by asset basis, or it may be an equal division in *total value* of the commonly owned property. Here are illustrations of both approaches.

EQUAL DIVISION OF INDIVIDUAL ASSETS

Marital property comprised of $40,000 savings, securities worth $30,000 consisting of 500 shares American Utility Corporation, and home worth $70,000, with no mortgage. All property jointly held.

If husband and wife were to divide the property so that each received $20,000 savings, 250 shares of American Utility, and a one-half interest in the home as tenants in common, this would be an equal division of each individual asset and the transfer of property under the settlement would not result in a tax to either spouse.

EQUAL DIVISION IN VALUE

Using the same property and value in the example above, the property could be divided so that the husband transfers his share of the home to the wife and the wife in turn transfers the securities and bank account to the husband. This would leave them in positions of equal value: the wife would have $70,000 real estate and the husband would have $30,000 securities plus $40,000 savings.

Since the division was equal in value, even though the individual assets were not divided equally, the settlement nevertheless would not give rise to a tax.

In either of the above examples, each spouse could keep his or her *separate* property, if agreed, and this by itself would not offset the tax consequences of the equal division of commonly owned property.

2. Figuring Gain or Loss on Sale

If there is an equal division of commonly owned property, each party will keep his or her original cost basis in the property. For example, say that husband and wife each paid $5,000 as his/her share of a $10,000 payment (no mortgage) for a summer home taken in joint names. If the home was later divided under a divorce settlement, each would have a "cost" for his or her share of $5,000, regardless of the value of the home at the time of settlement. The same result would apply if the husband paid the full $10,000, took the property in joint names and later transferred to his wife one-half the property in a divorce settlement, since one-half his original payment would be treated as if he made a gift of that amount to the wife at the time of purchase of the property.

In both examples, then, the wife's cost of the one-half interest in the summer home for tax purposes would be $5,000. If the home was later sold at $40,000 and she received one-half, or $20,000, she would be taxed on the $15,000 gain.

If the division of property is such that the husband receives certain assets while the wife receives others, the rule is a little more complicated but the effect is the same. The rule is that the transferee spouse will have a basis equal to the original cost (except where depreciable [business] property is involved).

For example, say that the husband purchased stock in joint names at a cost of $10,000 which is presently worth much more. As part of an *equal* division of property in a divorce settlement, he transfers the stock to his wife. She will have a cost in the stock of $10,000. Similarly, if he transferred only 40 percent of the stock to his wife as part of an equal division of property, she would have a cost of $4,000 in the 40 percent she received.

The reason for the nontaxability of the equal division is that each party is getting only that to which he or she is entitled and so no gain or loss is recognized at the time of settlement. If two people jointly own 100 shares of stock and they split it 50/50, neither has received more than his share. Caution should be exercised, however, in arbitrarily dividing commonly held property whenever there are marital problems. Free wheeling into and out of co-tenancies can have other tax implications (see Chapter 10), so expert advice should *always* be sought.

3. Treatment of Family Residence

Although the rules discussed above will apply to a transfer of the family's residence, special "negotiations" often accompany treatment of the residence and so it is given special attention here. For example, it may or may not be divided, and whether it is or not the wife may be allowed to continue to live there after the divorce. Here are some of the alternatives and the accompanying considerations:

HUSBAND TRANSFERS JOINTLY HELD RESIDENCE TO WIFE

If the transfer is part of an equal division as illustrated above, there will be no tax consequences to the husband. But if not, the transfer will be taxable to the husband under the Davis rule. His gain will be the fair value of one-half the house over his cost of one-half the house. For example, if he purchased the house for $40,000 and transfers his one-half interest to his wife when the house is worth $90,000, he would have a gain of $25,000. This is one-half the fair value of $90,000 less one-half the cost of $40,000 ($45,000 less $20,000 = $25,000.)

If the husband remains liable on the mortgage he will not be treated as having exchanged the property for its full fair value, so the amount of the mortgage will reduce his gain or even eliminate it. If the wife assumes (becomes responsible for) the mortgage, then the husband will be treated as receiving the full fair market value for his share of the home.

(Where the husband remains liable on the mortgage and continues to make payments on property that now belongs to the wife, he may be entitled to an income tax deduction for the mortgage payments as alimony to his wife, provided the agreement or divorce decree is consistent with this.)

HUSBAND KEEPS HIS ONE-HALF OF JOINTLY HELD RESIDENCE
BUT WIFE CONTINUES TO LIVE THERE.

If the home was originally held under a tenancy by the entirety
the divorce will render it a tenancy in common and husband and
wife would each own an undivided one-half interest in the home.
If it were originally a joint tenancy, it could remain that way after
the divorce. In *either* event, allowing the wife to stay there poses
no immediate tax problems to the husband (or the wife) since he is
giving up nothing except the right to possession.

If the husband pays the expenses, however, such as mortgage,
taxes, repairs, insurance, and so forth, then one-half of these payments could be deductible by him as alimony to his wife depending upon the agreement and decree. The half that applies to
his own interest in the property would not be deductible (except of
course for interest and taxes which are deductible in any event).
If the husband pays the utilities and does not live in the house,
these would generally be fully deductible by him (as alimony)
since they are for the sole benefit of the wife.

4. Gift Taxes

When a person transfers money or other property to another
without getting something of equal value in return, the tax laws
say a gift has been made and a gift tax may be imposed on the gift.
When one spouse transfers property (including joint property) to
the other for nothing more than a "relinquishment of marital
rights," is this a gift? It would be (and *can* be) were it not for the
following special rule: property transferred to a spouse in a divorce will not be subject to a gift tax, *provided* the property is
transferred in connection with a divorce decree or written settlement agreement of their marital rights or for support of minor
children, *and* the divorce occurs within two years after the date of
the agreement.

In other words, say that husband and wife, as a result of marital
problems, enter into a written agreement to divide property, and
in 1979 the husband proceeds to transfer a substantial amount of
property to his wife. Three years later they get a divorce. The
husband could be liable for a gift tax on the transfer of property

to his wife since the divorce did not occur within two years of the agreement.

This will *not* be a problem, however, and the rule *will not apply* to transfers made after December 31, 1981, because after that date no gift tax is imposed on gifts between husband and wife, regardless of the amount of the gift or the period of time between the gift and the divorce. However, *if there is no agreement* to divide the property and if a division of property occurs after the divorce (such as a tenancy by the entirety automatically becoming a tenancy in common after a divorce), then there *may* be a taxable gift, even after 1981, since the parties are no longer husband and wife.

5. Summary

This is not intended to be an exhaustive review of every tax ramification involved in divorce settlement, but rather merely of those important parts that relate to jointly held property. Because of the wide range of possible settlement arrangments, different state laws, and different circumstances of families and family property, the tax approach could vary from case to case. There are, however, two general rules that are very important to remember in considering any type of divorce settlement in which commonly held property may be involved.

First, a transfer of property from one spouse to another as part of a divorce or separation agreement can be taxable to the spouse making the transfer, even though he or she receives no money for the transfer.

Second, a critical exception to the first rule is that the transfer of property between spouses will not be taxable if it results in an equal division of the total value of the commonly owned property.

Finally, if you are involved in a divorce, be sure to get expert advice on the probable tax consequences of the proposed settlement before you accept it.

10

TAX PROBLEMS (AND BENEFITS) OF JOINT PROPERTY

INTRODUCTION

MOTHER OPENS A JOINT BANK account with daughter—who is taxed on the interest? Father purchases stock in joint names with son—has a taxable gift been made? Husband buys a vacation home jointly with his wife, then husband dies—is the property taxed in his estate? Each of these questions (and more, or course) can be asked in each situation. Often, however, none of these questions is asked until after the fact or until a serious tax problem has reared its ugly head.

If the legal ramifications of joint tenancy seem complicated, they pale in comparison to the tax considerations. Whenever you create or terminate an interest in joint property, you should be aware of the potential tax problems (and the potential tax benefits) in three basic areas: income tax, gift tax, and estate tax. This chapter deals with the general problems in each of these categories when different types of jointly held property are involved. (Tax complications relating to divorce settlements with joint property are covered separately in Chapter 9.) The intention here is not to make you a tax expert but rather to give you a general understanding of the basic tax concepts related to joint ownership.

Further, the discussions in this chapter apply for the most part to a tenancy by the entirety as well as to a joint tenancy, except in those states that still recognize the *common law* concept of the tenancy by the entirety (see Chapter 4). This somewhat anti-quated concept holds that where husband and wife hold property under a tenancy by the entirety, the husband has the *sole* right to income from the property during his life. In these states, the *husband* will be entitled to and taxed on such income. Some states, although they still recognize the designation "tenancy by the entirety," have enacted laws that give the couple *equal rights* over income and possession of the property. In these states, each spouse would be taxed on his or her share of the income. Of course, if the couples file a joint return it will make no difference from an income tax standpoint. And from an estate tax stand-point the tax laws make no major distinction between the tenancy by the entirety and the joint tenancy. However, any other im-portant differences will be noted.

As to the tenancy in common, the discussions in this chapter, with one exception, do *not* apply to a tenancy in common, since *for tax purposes each tenant in common is treated as if he individ-ually owned his share of the property.* The exception is with re-spect to gift taxes. Transfer of property into a tenancy in common or changing title from a joint tenancy (or tenancy by the entirety) to a tenancy in common could result in a taxable gift, as pointed out in Section 2 of this chapter.

Finally, although tax considerations are the focus of this chapter, it must be noted that many (but not all) of the tax results are based on the *legal* relationship of the parties (so if you haven't already read Chapters 2–5, better do so now). For example, it may be that dividends on jointly held stock are taxed equally to each of the joint owners, on account of the legal right of each to cause a severance of the property and take his share. On the other hand, the tax results for one purpose may not be consistent with the tax results for another purpose. Continued example: even though dividends on jointly held stock of mother and daughter are (for income tax purposes) taxed half to the mother and half to the daughter, it will not necessarily follow that on mother's (or daughter's) death, only half of the stock will be subject to estate tax. Further, some tax results could differ depending upon whether the joint tenants were married or not. Confused yet? Read on.

1. INCOME TAXES AND JOINT PROPERTY

AS A GENERAL RULE, WHEN two or more individuals own property jointly, each is entitled to an equal share of the income (or loss) generated by that property. Consequently, each will be taxed on his share of the income, whether or not actually taken. For example, if two people jointly own shares of a mutual fund that declared an annual dividend of $600, each joint owner would show a $300 dividend on his tax return even though the dividend might have been "reinvested" in additional shares by the joint owners.

Tax questions on income from joint property would be fairly easy if the general rule always applied. Unfortunately, there are several important exceptions to the general rule. The exceptions are best illustrated by applying the income tax rules to each of the common types of property or joint ownership arrangements: joint bank accounts, jointly held securities, jointly held United States Savings Bonds, and jointly held real estate.

A. JOINT BANK ACCOUNTS

In spite of their overwhelming popularity, joint bank accounts as a general rule do not fall under the general rule. Sound confusing? It is, because the income tax consequences depend upon "local" law, and this will differ from state to state. That is, the law of the state in which the bank account is located will determine who is taxed on the interest. If the state law provides that each joint owner has a right to an equal share of the *income,* then this is how the IRS will tax it. On the other hand, if state law says there is no such right, then the interest will be taxed in proportion to the *contribution* of each joint owner. So in such states, if mother opens an account with her funds and adds daughter's name as joint owner, mother alone will be taxed since the entire contribution came from her.

As seen in Chapter 7, the majority of states hold that the non-contributing joint tenant of a joint bank account has no right to the funds until there has been some clear indication that the contributing joint tenant intends the other to have a true joint interest in the account. This is often difficult to prove and so gives rise to income tax questions as to who is taxed. When there is any doubt, however, the IRS will usually tax the joint tenants in proportion to their contributions to the account.

Some accounts have so much activity in deposits and withdrawals that it may be difficult to tell who contributed what. In this case, the joint tenants themselves would have to make their best guess at the proportions of their contributions and report the interest accordingly. If you can't figure out the shares, the IRS probably can't either.

Speaking of reporting the interest, the bank tells the IRS how much you earned on your account by tagging it to the "tax identification number" you give when opening the account. For most of us, this is our social security number. On a joint account between husband and wife, it is the *husband's* social security number that is generally required (no comment). However, on accounts for joint tenants who are other than husband and wife you are supposed to give the number of the contributing joint tenant. If both are contributors you should give both numbers and instruct the bank to report the interest accordingly. As a result of this system of reporting, many people are led to believe that the interest can legally be taxed according to the social security number used rather than the contribution made. Frequently, mother will put daughter's social security number on the bank account in an effort to have the interest taxed to daughter, even though mother was the sole contributor and retains full control and enjoyment of the funds. This won't work. Or perhaps it may be more accurate to say, this will work until mother gets caught!

Remember, the identification number is just that, a means of identification. It has no legal effect and cannot *legally* shift the tax burden from one person to another.

Husband-and-wife joint bank accounts are, you guessed it, subject to special rules in many cases. The rules, unfortunately, vary from state to state and depend to some degree upon whether a particular state has enacted laws specifically relating to treatment of joint bank accounts. The following two positions are predominant.

Those states that still recognize the common law tenancy by the entirety may treat husband-and-wife joint bank accounts as a tenancy by the entirety (Massachusetts, for example) even though the title of the account suggests it is joint. In some states this could mean that the husband is entitled to all the income (interest) earned on the account. It could be argued, however, that the tenancy is modified by the contract with the bank or by the actions of the parties themselves. But if there is a question, the current local law should be checked because of the rapidly changing nature of the law dealing with the marital relationship.

This may not appear to be of great importance when, as far as you can see, the joint account seems to work the same whether you're married or not. It could make an important difference, however, when someone else—a creditor, for example—is interested in your account. If a creditor of the wife attempts to reach a joint bank account in a state where the account is treated as a tenancy by the entirety, the creditor may find that she has no "interest" in the account that is reachable by him.

The second major position taken by many states for husband-and-wife joint bank accounts is the presumption that when such an account is created, a gift is made to the noncontributing spouse, resulting in an equal share for each. This is discussed in more detail in Chapter 7, but in effect the presumption makes the account a true joint account, resulting in each being taxed on his or her share of the income. This is so even though one joint tenant may take or use more of the income than the other. But where husband and wife file a joint income tax return, this would make no difference since their income is combined on the return. However, in those states where joint income returns are not allowed or where husband and wife are not allowed to split income, then the interest on the joint bank account will be taxed one-half to each.

Overall, the two distinctions discussed above do not create the need for any particular action on the part of a husband and wife who have a joint bank account, but they are nevertheless important to know when taxation of the account is being considered.

To summarize, if each joint owner has a legal right under state law to a share of the account, then each will be taxed on his share of the interest earned. If, on the other hand, a true joint tenancy does not exist, or it is a form of convenience account as described in Chapter 7, then the interest will be taxed in proportion to the contributions made to the account by each joint owner. The social security number on the account has no legal effect and cannot by itself determine who will be taxed on the interest.

B. JOINTLY HELD SECURITIES

Income taxes on securities are a little clearer than those on joint bank accounts. Once securities (stocks, bonds, or promissory notes) are *registered* in joint names, each joint tenant has a right of severance as detailed in Chapter 5, and therefore *each will be taxed on his proportional share of the dividends, interest, or capital gains (or losses)* as the case may be, regardless of the source of funds used to purchase the securities. (The gift tax implications are discussed later in this chapter.)

For example, Dad buys 100 shares of stock and registers the stock in the names of himself, son, and daughter as joint tenants. The stock pays $300 in dividends. Each of the three joint tenants will show $100 of dividends on his tax return. If the stock is later sold at a $3,000 gain, each will show a $1,000 capital gain on his tax return.

There may be considerable income tax advantages to shifting dividends to lower-bracket taxpayers by registering securities jointly with them. However, there are other factors that must also be considered, for example, the gift tax question. A taxable gift may have occurrred on registration of the securities and the fact that the other joint tenant or tenants now have a right to a share of the securities.

For married couples who file a joint return, there are no income tax advantages except for any allowable dividend exclusions.

Note that the above discussion refers to securities that have been *registered* in joint names. In many instances a joint brokerage account is opened, and although securities may be purchased through this joint account, they are not registered but remain with the broker in "street" name. This is a critical point and must be determined if an income tax question arises. Street name is the term used for securities that are retained in the name of the brokerage firm itself (for ease of transfer) and *not* in the names of the actual owners. Unfortunately, at this writing it is not clear whether income from securities held in street name will be taxed to each of the joint tenants or just to the contributing joint tenant in proportion to his or her contributions. In effect, a street name account may be treated like a joint bank account when the contributions are unequal. That is, until a completed interest has been transferred or established under local law, only the contributors are taxed. Once again, local law can have an important bearing on the tax consequences.

If the local law states that each joint tenant has a legal right to an equal share of the account, then each will be taxed accordingly on the dividends, interest, or capital gains. This is not always an easy thing to establish. It should not be left to question. If you decide that you want each joint tenant to be taxed on his share of the income, then have the securities registered or make it clear in some other way (a letter or agreement) that this is the intent. It could save taxes and trouble later on.

C. JOINTLY HELD SAVINGS BONDS

The United States currently issues two types of savings bonds—Series EE and Series HH, although many of the older Series E and Series H bonds are still outstanding. The EE and HH bonds are merely new versions of the earlier Series E and H, and all of these bonds are treated the same for income tax purposes. EE bonds are issued at a discount but are redeemable at face value when they mature. HH bonds are issued at face value and pay interest semiannually until they mature.

From the standpoint of joint tenancy, any of the above bonds may be held in the names of "A and B," or "A or B," but this should not be confused with the allowable (and popular) designation of a beneficiary on death, such as "Mary Bove payable on death to Adrienne Bove," which is *not* a form of co-tenancy.

United States bonds (Series E or H or EE or HH) that are registered in joint names are subject to special rules. Interest on these bonds is taxed *according to contribution,* regardless of local law and regardless of the fact that they have been registered in joint names. As a result, there are generally no income tax advantages to holding those bonds in joint names.

If Series E or Series EE bonds that are in joint names (purchased by one of the joint tenants) are subsequently re-registered in the single name of the *non*contributing joint tenant, the joint tenant who purchased the bonds will at that time be taxed on the interest accrued to the date of the re-registration. If the re-registration conforms to the contributions of each joint owner, then no tax will result.

For example, if the mother purchases some Series EE bonds in the names of herself and her daughter, jointly, when the bonds are cashed in, all the interest will be taxable to the mother. If prior to redeeming the bonds, the mother has the bonds re-registered so that they are now only in *her* name, then no tax will result since the full contribution was made by the mother and the new registration is now in her name alone. But if she re-registers them solely in daughter's name, then mother will be taxed on the interest earned up to the date of the re-registration and daughter, the new owner of the bonds, will be taxed on all interest earned *after* that date. Further, when daughter became the owner of the bonds, she received a gift from her mother, as discussed later in this chapter.

D. JOINTLY HELD REAL ESTATE

There is something special about real estate as compared to all other types of property. It just seems to have more permanence and significance than, say, stocks or bonds or even gold. One factor that adds to this aura is the formality with which real estate is handled—deeds with precise descriptions, signed and sworn to before a notary, then permanently recorded at the official registry as a formal certification of the transaction.

All this fanfare about real estate is carried through in the legal and tax results when it is placed in joint names. Once again, however, special rules apply to husband and wife, and therefore this is treated separately below.

1. Income (and Deductions) for Joint Owners Other Than Husband and Wife

When real estate is owned jointly by two or more persons, the income it produces will be taxed to each of the co-owners in proportion to his share. This applies not only to rents or other profits generated from the property but to a sale of the property as well. Thus, a considerable income tax savings could result from a sharing of the income.

For example, Mr. B. purchases rental property for $60,000 with a deposit of $10,000 and a $50,000 mortgage. He takes title in the joint names of himself and his adult son, who also becomes liable on the mortgage. The property generates taxable income of $2,000 per year, of which $1,000 will be taxed to Mr. B and $1,000 to his son. Any depreciation allowed on the property will likewise be split according to ownership. Other deductions, however, may be treated differently. If Mr. B pays all the interest on the real estate he will be entitled to deduct these amounts on his tax return, while his son will not. If they each pay a share of the interest and taxes, each will be able to deduct the amount he paid. Therefore, the deductions for these items *may or may not be equal* depending upon who pays them.

Say that a year or more later the property is sold for $71,000, giving them about $12,000 profit (after adding back about $1,000 for depreciation taken). The profit would be taxed $6,000 to Mr. B and $6,000 to his son. Similarly, if the property were sold at a loss, the loss would be deductible one-half by each.

Be careful not to make this type of transfer into joint names just prior to a sale in an effort to have the profits taxed in a lower bracket. The IRS may very likely treat this as a sale by the original owner *before* the transfer and then as subsequent taxable gifts to the new joint owners—a costly result.

Also, caution should be observed when children are considered since in most states minors cannot own real estate, or if they do, a purchaser cannot obtain good title from the minor. As a result, a guardianship usually becomes necessary to "hold" the minor's interest in the property. Further, transfers of income-producing property to a minor (dependent) child may affect the dependency exemption allowed the parent. This should be considered before making any transfers to shift income.

Where the co-owners are not jointly liable on the mortgage, the income tax rules discussed above will still apply, but payment of the mortgage by one could result in gift tax implications to the other as discussed later in this chapter.

2. Income Tax Treatment for Husband and Wife

There is generally no *income tax* advantage for a married couple to own real estate jointly unless they file *separate* income tax returns rather than a joint return, since filing jointly has the effect of splitting the income of husband and wife—the same tax effect as joint ownership of the income-producing property.

In those rare cases when the husband and wife are filing separately, it may make a difference how the income-producing property is held since each will report his or her share. For example, if the property is held under a tenancy by the entirety in a state that recognizes the common law form of that tenancy, it may be that the husband will be taxed on all of the income. In such states, there would be no income-splitting advantage unless a separate return were filed.

E. HOW THE SURVIVING JOINT OWNER IS TAXED ON SALE OF THE PROPERTY

When a surviving joint owner sells or exchanges the property he now holds as sole owner, special rules apply in determining his gain or loss. As with any gain or loss, the seller's cost "basis" must be established. In the simplest case the basis is the actual cost or price paid for the property. With joint property, however, it may be that the surviving joint owner paid nothing for the property. He simply owns it by right of survivorship.

If the surviving joint owner acquired the property through his right of survivorship and through no contribution of his own, then his basis is determined by the value of the property in the deceased joint owner's estate, to the extent it was included in the estate, even though the actual *cost* of the property may have been more or less than the estate tax value.

For example, Jonnie purchases securities for $10,000 with his own funds and has them registered jointly with his friend, Willie. On Jonnie's death the stocks are worth $25,000 (and they are reported at this value on Jonnie's estate tax return) and Willie is now the sole owner by right of survivorship. Later, Willie sells the stocks at a price of $26,000. Under these facts, Willie's cost basis is $25,000 and he has a $1,000 taxable gain on the sale. Further, it doesn't matter how long Willie holds the stock after Jonnie's death, the gain will be long term, says the Internal Revenue Code.

If the surviving joint tenant had contributed to the purchase price of the joint property, then his contribution is of course added to his cost basis for the property. If he received the property by gift, then his cost will be the same cost as it was for the person who gave him the gift (with certain adjustments if a gift tax was paid).

If he paid for half and inherited the other half when his co-tenant died, then his cost will be the amount he paid plus the value of the other one-half in the estate of the deceased co-tenant. For example, in the above illustration, say that Jonnie and Willie each paid $5,000 for the stocks. On Jonnie's death, only one-half would be included (since Willie owned and paid for the other half) and say that the value of *one-half* at death was $12,500. Therefore, Willie's new cost basis in the stocks would be $5,000 (the cost of his share) plus $12,500 (the value of Jonnie's share in his estate) or a total of $17,500. If he then sold them for $26,000, he would have a gain of $8,500.

If the property involved is depreciable or business property or subject to other special tax treatment, then the computations will be a bit more complicated, but the basic conception as stated above will still apply.

F. INCOME TAX SUMMARY

Income from jointly owned real estate and jointly registered securities will be taxed equally to the joint owners. Interest on United States Series E bonds, when taxed, will be taxed to the person who paid for them until they are re-registered in another name or the name of the noncontributing joint owner. Income from joint bank accounts and joint brokerage accounts (in street name, as opposed to registered securities) will be taxed according to contributions to the account, unless state law provides otherwise, and it usually does if the joint owners are husband and wife. Gains or losses on a sale of jointly registered securities or real estate will be taxed to (or deductible by) each of the joint owners equally.

A sale of the joint property by a surviving joint owner (after the death of his co-tenant) is subject to special rules, but basically his gain or loss will be dependent on the extent to which the joint property is included in the deceased joint owner's estate and the value it is given for estate tax purposes.

Remember that income tax is only one of the areas that must be considered, and that the income tax results are not necessarily consistent with the gift tax or estate tax results. Each area must be compared and reviewed before drawing any final conclusions.

2. GIFT TAXES AND JOINT PROPERTY

DEPENDING UPON THE TYPE OF co-tenancy and the nature of the transfer itself, placing property in any one of the three popular types of co-tenancies (joint tenancy, tenancy by the entirety, and tenancy in common) could result in a taxable gift, if the contributions of the co-tenants are different from their shares in the common property. This result often comes as a surprise to both the donor (the person making the gift) and the donee (the recipient of the gift).

A discussion of the complex and far-reaching implications of gifts and gift taxes—even limited to co-tenancies—is beyond the scope and intent of this book. Rather, the objective is to familiarize you with the potential problems and give you a basic understanding of the principles involved to help avoid such problems in the future. To begin with, a bare-bones discussion of gifts and gift taxes follows, so when we say that a "taxable gift" has been made, you'll know what this means.

A. BASICS OF GIFTS AND GIFT TAXES

Although several states have a gift tax, this discussion is limited to the *federal* gift tax laws and regulations. The Internal Revenue Code imposes a tax on all lifetime gifts made from one individual to another. This is the basic rule and were it not for certain exemptions and/or deductions, *all* gifts would be subject to a federal gift tax.

The first and perhaps the most popular exemption from the tax is the $10,000 annual exclusion (prior to 1982 this was a *$3,000* annual exclusion). To qualify for this the gift must be presently enjoyable by the donee. In other words, with the exception of special minor's trusts, the donee must not have to wait to enjoy the gift. The annual exclusion applies on a "per donee" basis and may be used over and over again each year. A donor, then, may make as many $10,000 gifts as he likes to different individuals each year, without limitation. In addition, a donor's spouse may allow the donor to use her or his $10,000 exclusion, so each donee could receive as much as $20,000 per year before a taxable gift would result.

The $10,000 exclusion from gift taxes is the *only* gift tax break allowed, except for gifts between spouses discussed below. Although prior to 1977 there was a $30,000 "lifetime exemption," this has been *repealed*. Therefore, when Dad (alone) gives son a $12,000 car in 1982, he has made a *taxable* gift of $2,000 ($12,000 less $10,000 exclusion). The federal gift tax on a taxable gift of $2,000 is $360.

But Dad may not have to actually pay this, since he, like everyone else, is entitled to a gift tax *credit* of $62,800 (for 1982) and he will apply a part of this credit to offset the gift tax. This credit is called a "unified" credit, because it applies to gift taxes as well as estate taxes. The credit increases each year until 1987 when it reaches $192,800.

Under the present tax rate tables, a credit of $62,800 corresponds to a gift (or estate) of about $225,000, while the credit for 1987 and thereafter will correspond to gifts or an estate totaling $600,000. This means that the credit will eliminate the tax on that amount.

Gifts Between Spouses

As usual there are special rules for gifts between spouses. The rules have been somewhat simplified after 1981 and basically provide that there will be *no tax* on gifts between spouses after that date, regardless of the amount of the gift. This is known as an unlimited gift tax marital deduction.

For gifts during 1981 and prior, some very complicated rules applied. Some gifts between spouses (those over $100,000) could produce a gift tax, and special elections applied to joint property and jointly held business interests. These have been repealed, however, with the 1981 Economic Recovery Tax Act.

Value of the Gift

For purposes of computing the gift tax on the amount of the gift, the law requires you use the fair market value of the gift on the date the gift was made, regardless of the cost of the gift to the donor. However, for *income* tax purposes, the donee takes the donor's cost of the gift, as a general rule. For example, mother gives daughter securities presently worth $10,000 but which cost mother only $2,000. Mother has made a $10,000 gift to daughter, but daughter has a cost basis in the securities of only $2,000, so that if she immediately sells them, she'll have a capital gain of $8,000.

Gifts Not Tax Deductible

Be sure you understand the distinction between gifts and income taxes. They are unrelated. Gifts to individuals are *not* deductible on your income tax return, nor are they taxable to the donee.

Warning: This is not a detailed study of the federal gift tax laws. It is a brief discussion of some of the basics and should by no means be used to make gifts without consulting a tax advisor. It is offered merely to help you better understand the potential gift tax considerations where joint tenancies are created or terminated in the various types of property.

B. JOINT BANK ACCOUNTS—GIFT TAX IMPLICATIONS

As a general rule, no gift results when one person deposits funds in a joint bank account with another. However, when the noncontributing joint owner withdraws funds, a gift occurs of the amount withdrawn, unless the withdrawing co-owner has a legal obligation to account to the other for the money taken (like a loan). In other words, if one simply allows the other to withdraw funds, with the understanding that he will never have to repay, then a gift has been made.

A gift of the bankbook to the noncontributing joint tenant, unaccompanied by a withdrawal, may or may not constitute a gift, depending on all the facts and circumstances surrounding the transfer, and the laws of the particular state involved. As a general rule, however, a gift of the book with the intention that the donee have the funds is strong evidence in favor of a gift.

Some states' laws have the effect of creating a gift of one-half the balance in the account as soon as the joint account is opened, because of the rights of each joint tenant to withdraw an equal share. As a practical matter, however, gifts and gift taxes are a relatively minor problem where joint bank accounts are concerned. The big problems are really nontax and center on the question of who gets the money, as discussed in Chapter 7.

C. JOINTLY HELD SECURITIES

Since securities often play such an important role in a family's investment plans, and because joint ownership (right or wrong) seems to play an equally important role, securities are frequently held in joint names by various family members. As a general rule, when securities *are registered* in joint names and the funds used to purchase securities are not contributed equally by the joint owners, a gift will result. For example, John pays $30,000 for securities, which he has registered in his and Mary's name, jointly. He has made a gift of $15,000 to Mary. Further, if Mary decides to turn them back over to John, she would be making another gift of $15,000 to John.

These rules apply only if the securities have been *registered* in joint names and the noncontributing joint tenant gains legal rights to his share of the securities. When securities (or cash) are held in a brokerage account in street name (the name of the brokerage firm and not the joint owners), the IRS generally does not treat them as a gift to the noncontributing tenant. It is treated for gift tax purposes similar to a joint bank account, where a gift normally occurs only when the noncontributing joint tenant *withdraws* funds (or in this case securities) from the account. The value of the gift will be the value of the securities (or money) withdrawn from the account for the benefit of the noncontributing joint tenant.

Although this rule may seem to offer a break from the gift tax treatment, it could lead to problems in the future. For example, say that Sam, with his funds, purchases $20,000 of securities in a joint brokerage account with Elaine, leaving the securities in street name. (Having them registered would have resulted in a $10,000 gift.) Many years later the securities in the account are worth $150,000. A registration at that point would result in a $75,000 gift to Elaine. It may not be possible to predict the growth of any joint account, but once it is known that certain action may result in a taxable gift, it is quite possible to avoid that action.

D. JOINTLY HELD UNITED STATES SAVINGS BONDS

United States savings bonds registered in joint names do not follow the rule of jointly registered securities as discussed above. If one person purchases a United States savings bond and has it registered in his name and another's as joint tenants he has not made a gift. However, if the bond is re-registered in the sole name of the noncontributing tenant who receives all or a part of the proceeds, a gift will occur. Of course, if the donor purchases a bond in the joint names of persons other than himself (A purchases bonds in the names of B and C) then a gift has clearly been made to the new owners of the bond.

In any event, the value of the gift will be the redemption value of the bond at the time of the gift or the amount of the proceeds received by the donee.

E. JOINTLY HELD REAL ESTATE—OTHER THAN HUSBAND AND WIFE

As with jointly held securities, a gift will result when real estate is taken in joint names and one party pays or contributes more than his share. This problem arises quite frequently after the death of one spouse when the surviving spouse will then place the property in joint names with a child.

For example, after father's death, mother transfers the real estate she inherited from him over to herself and her son, jointly, since she wants him to receive it "if anything should happen to her." At the time of the transfer, the property was worth $80,000 and there was no mortgage. Mother has made a $40,000 gift to son.

The reason is that mother has irrevocably given son a one-half interest in the property. She cannot recover this interest without her son's cooperation. Son, in fact, could have a court order the property sold so he could take his one-half share (the right of partition as described in Chapter 5). Such as an absolute transfer would clearly constitute a gift.

If the parties were husband and wife, the exposure to gifts is academic, because as pointed out above, each may make unlimited gifts to the other (after 1981) without exposure to a gift tax. Even where other parties are concerned, gifts will have to be pretty large before a gift tax is actually due because of the sizable tax credit allowed. However, it is still important to understand when a gift has been made because it may have a bearing on estate taxes as discussed later in this chapter.

In short, when a person purchases real estate with his own funds, or already owns real estate and has the title made out to himself and another (or others) as joint tenants, there is an immediate gift from the owner to the other joint tenant of his equal share of the property.

Mortgaged Property

The amount of any mortgage would be subtracted from the value or purchase price of the property to determine the "equity." It is the joint tenant's share of the equity that is the amount of the gift. For example, if Fred purchases real estate for $50,000 with a deposit of $10,000 and a mortgage of $40,000, then has title transferred to himself and Ruth as joint tenants, he has made a gift to Ruth of only $5,000 (one half the equity of $10,000).

Payments on the mortgage may also be gifts if they are all made by one of the tenants. In the above example, say that during the year Ruth made all the mortgage payments, reducing the balance on the mortgage by $4,000. If this happened she would have made a gift to Fred of $2,000. (Remember, however, that gifts of $10,000 or less to a person in any one year are not a problem for gift tax purposes. And where the $10,000 exclusion is exceeded so that a gift tax is due, the donor will then use any allowable gift tax credit on the excess.)

Ending the Joint Tenancy

The results of terminating the joint tenancy in real estate are similar to those where registered securities are involved. If either tenant ends up with less than his equal share, a gift has been made. It can be risky, for example, to try to rectify a previously made gift in joint tenancy by transferring the property back to the original owner. Another gift can result! To illustrate, dad purchases $50,000 of real estate (no mortgage) and takes title jointly with son. He has made a $25,000 gift to son at this time. Later, when the property is worth $80,000, dad decides to sell the property, but just before the sale has son transfer the property back in dad's name alone. Son has now made a gift of $40,000 to dad. If there were a mortgage on the property, the gifts in either case would be reduced by the joint tenant's "share" of the mortgage. That is, the gift would apply only to the equity in the property.

F. GIFT TAX SUMMARY

When any property is placed in the joint names of two or more individuals and each of them does not contribute an equal share, a gift has probably been made for federal gift tax purposes. There are, of course, some exceptions to this—joint bank accounts, United States savings bonds, and brokerage accounts in street name are subject to special considerations. Further, any property owned or taken jointly (or as tenants by the entirety) by husband and wife (unless given to them by someone else) does not present a gift tax problem because of the unlimited gift tax marital deduction that applies to gifts (from one spouse to another) made after 1981.

The consequence of making a gift for tax purposes may not be as disastrous as it sounds. As pointed out in the beginning of this chapter, the fact that a gift has been made does not necessarily mean that a gift tax may be due. Gifts between husbands and wives enjoy special tax breaks and present gifts to other individuals of up to $10,000 per person per year completely escape the gift tax. And on any gift that is taxable, we may apply our allowable credit.

3. ESTATE TAXES AND JOINT PROPERTY

A. INTRODUCTION

If it weren't for section 2040 of the Internal Revenue Code, property that is held in joint names would never be taxed in anyone's estate. The Code's basic approach to estate taxes is centered on the *interest* (in any property) the decedent possessed or retained at his death. Where joint property is concerned, this definition would fail to include it, because on the death of a joint tenant, he has *no* interest or rights in the property—they belong to the survivor—therefore, there is technically nothing to tax in his estate.

Quickly noting the potential revenue loss such a result would cause, Congress adopted section 2040 of the Internal Revenue Code, which operates to include *all* the jointly held property in the estate of a deceased joint tenant, subject, of course, to certain exceptions. The first part of this section will offer a broad overview of estate taxes so you can judge the effect of including the joint property as explained further on.

In the estate tax discussions that follow, specific types of property—real estate, securities, etc.—are not dealt with individually (as was necessary with gift taxes) since the rules and principles of law covered apply to all types of jointly held property.

B. ESTATE TAXES—AN OVERVIEW

Provisions of the Internal Revenue Code go to great lengths to include in your estate the value of any and all property with which you are even remotely connected, and even some property with which you feel you have given up all connections. This is not to say that nothing escapes estate taxes but rather to orient you to the attitude of the tax laws so as to help increase your general understanding of them and to reduce the surprises that result from misunderstanding.

One of the more popular misunderstandings is that joint property is not subject to estate tax in the estate of a deceased joint owner. In fact, the presumption created by the tax code is just the *opposite* as we shall see. Further, inclusion in the taxable estate may or may not be a problem, depending upon the overall size of the deceased's estate. In fact, most estates in this country will pay little or no federal estate tax. Let's take a look at the basics.

Every estate is entitled to a federal estate tax *credit* of $47,000 (for deaths in 1981). A tax *credit* differs from a tax *deduction* in that the credit can be applied dollar for dollar against the tax due, while a deduction operates to reduce the amount on which the tax is computed. In terms of estate size, a $47,000 tax credit is equal to an estate of about $175,000. Therefore, if a person dies with an estate valued at $175,000 there will be no federal estate tax.

What's more, this credit increases each year through 1987, as follows:

YEAR	ALLOWABLE TAX CREDIT	CREDIT EQUAL TO AN ESTATE OF
1982	$ 62,800	$225,000
1983	$ 79,300	$275,000
1984	$ 96,300	$325,000
1985	$121,800	$400,000
1986	$155,800	$500,000
1987 and after	$192,800	$600,000

In addition to the estate tax credit, the estate may be entitled to a "marital deduction." This is a *deduction* from the amount of the estate subject to tax and applies to property that passes to the deceased's surviving spouse. The maximum marital deduction that is allowed is equal to *all* amounts that pass to a surviving spouse in a manner that qualifies for the deduction with no limit. These amounts will pass tax-free to a surviving spouse. There is much more to the marital deduction than the preceding few sentences. However, there should be enough to understand that property passing to a surviving spouse by reason of joint property or property held under a tenancy by the entirety with the surviving spouse *will qualify* for the marital deduction and, in general, it may pass to the surviving spouse free of federal estate taxes.

For example, if the entire estate of Mary and Marvin consists of jointly held real estate worth $80,000 and jointly held securities worth $170,000, on Marvin's death the full $250,000 may pass to Mary free of federal estate taxes on account of the marital deduction. As another example, take an extreme case, where Henry and Henrietta have $20 million in jointly held stock (a bad idea if you didn't already know it). On Henry's death the entire $20 million can pass to Henrietta free of federal estate taxes on account of the unlimited marital deduction.

Whether or not the full amount of the joint property will be included in the estate depends upon many factors. There are basic rules and exceptions as discussed below, but it must be kept in mind that they apply *only to joint tenancies and tenancies by the entirety*—they do not apply to tenancies in common.

C. THE GENERAL RULE

The basic position taken by the Internal Revenue Code is that *the full value of all the joint property in which the deceased was a joint tenant is included in the estate of the deceased* for federal estate tax purposes.

As pointed out above, the application of this rule may or may not present a tax problem, depending on the size of the estate. However, the Code is not really interested in whether the rule helps or hurts you—it shoots first and asks questions later. This approach can present problems if the surviving joint tenants are not aware of it or of the exceptions that may help save taxes.

Exceptions to the General Rule

There are three exceptions to the general rule of including the entire amount of the joint property in the estate. They are:

1. The "consideration-furnished" test. Under this exception, if the surviving joint tenant can show that some or all of the joint property was purchased by him or attributable to his contribution, then that proportion of the value will be excluded from the deceased's estate. This test will not apply to property held by husband and wife under a joint tenancy or a tenancy by the entirety.

2. The "gift or inheritance" test. If the surviving joint tenant can show that the joint property was given to the joint owners by some third party or that the property was inherited by them

jointly, then only the deceased tenant's equal share will be included in his estate.

3. The "husband and wife" test. If the jointly held property (including a tenancy by the entirety) is held only by husband and wife, then only one-half the value of that property will be included in the estate of the deceased joint owner for tax purposes.

Contributions by Surviving Joint Owner

[Remember, after 1981 this test is not necessary for husband and wife joint tenants.] Where the joint tenancy was created by one or more of the joint tenants, the estate (or the surviving joint tenant) must show what amount of consideration (for acquiring the property) was furnished by the surviving joint tenant or tenants. If it cannot be shown to the satisfaction of the IRS that the survivor furnished the funds (or if one of the other exceptions doesn't apply), the general rule will bring the *full amount* of the joint property into the estate.

Proof of contribution is a constant problem for estates and for surviving joint owners. If the joint tenants fail to keep track of who contributed what over the years, it is difficult, if not impossible, for a surviving joint owner to prove any contribution even though in fact there was some. In some cases, acceptable proof may be in the form of "circumstantial" evidence—that is, by the surviving joint owner showing that he or she worked for a certain number of years, produced a certain amount of income which was commingled with the deceased joint owner's funds and used to purchase the joint property, so there *must* have been some contribution. Under this approach, if the survivor's earnings were 30 percent of the total earnings, he or she may be successful in excluding 30 percent of the value from the estate. [Once again, this rule does *not* apply where husband and wife are the joint tenants and death occurs after 1981.]

In any case, if you must have joint property, it is essential that you keep some records as to the source of the funds used to purchase the property. Such records might include not only your own "diary" detailing the source, but check stubs, bank deposits with notes as to what was deposited, broker's confirmations on sales of securities, etc. These records must be kept until the death of a joint owner, and this could entail a period of many years. If there are no such records or evidence to be found, you may file an "affidavit of a surviving joint owner," which is a sworn statement outlining your position as to the contribution you furnished. If submitted without any supporting evidence, it may or may not be accepted by the IRS as proof of contribution. In one case, the United States Tax Court accepted oral testimony from the widow of a deceased joint owner as to her contribution to the joint property, but this is a relatively rare situation. In any event, if there was contribution, some effort should be made to show it, even if only by the filing of an affidavit.

Tracing the Funds Sometimes, what you may feel is your contribution is not the way the IRS or the tax law sees it. If the funds used to purchase the joint property can be traced back to the deceased, then the property will be included in his estate, even though it appears the funds came from someone else. For example, dad makes a gift of $10,000 cash to his daughter. A few years later they decide to purchase some securities and each puts up $10,000 (daughter uses the money she received from dad earlier). They purchase $20,000 of securities in joint names and sometime later dad dies. Under the consideration-furnished test, dad is considered to have furnished *all* the consideration, and so the full value of the securities will be included in his estate, because the funds used by the surviving joint owner can be traced back to the deceased. If this were not the rule, the consideration-furnished test would be easily circumvented by giving cash to the other joint tenant who would then use the funds to purchase a "share" of the joint property.

There is, however, a favorable twist to this situation. You remember that joint tenants are each taxed on their individual share of the *income* from the joint property even though the property was a gift from the other joint tenant. Since the income belongs to each joint tenant equally, it is treated as the individual joint tenant's own property. Following this line of reasoning, the tax regulations state that the tracing requirement applies only to the *principal* and not to the *income*. Using the above example of dad and daughter, it might work like this: daughter takes the $10,000 gift from dad and invests it in securities paying a 15 percent dividend ($1,500 per year). Two years later she takes the $3,000 she "earned" and uses it to purchase her share of $6,000 worth of securities jointly with dad. On dad's subsequent death, only one-half of the $6,000 in jointly held securities will be included in his estate because daughter can be shown to have contributed the other half through her share of the *income*.

Therefore, using the *income* from the joint or gift property will avoid having the subsequently purchased joint property brought back into the estate under the tracing requirement.

Successful Proof of Contribution If you are successful in proving to the IRS that the surviving joint tenant contributed some portion of the purchase price of the joint property and that the funds or property cannot be traced to the deceased joint owner as discussed above, then that portion of the joint property in question will be excluded from the deceased's estate. That is, the exclusion is not on a dollar amount but on a *proportional* amount based on contribution.

For example, Bruce and Bob purchase $10,000 of property, taking title as joint tenants. Of the purchase price, Bruce pays $8,000 and Bob pays $2,000, each from his personal funds. Bob dies at a time when the property is worth $30,000, and only $6,000 (20 percent of $30,000) will be included in his estate. The balance of $24,000 (80 percent) will be excluded as the proportionate contribution of the surviving joint owner, Bruce.

THE GIFT OR INHERITANCE TEST

When the property in question was inherited by or given to the deceased joint tenant and the other joint tenant by some *third party* (not one of the surviving joint tenants), then only the deceased's share is included in his estate. There is no need to prove contribution (since there may have been none) but it *is* necessary to prove that the joint property was the subject of a gift or inheritance.

For example, mother dies and leaves her home to son and daughter as joint tenants. On son's subsequent death only one-half the value of the home will be included in his estate, since his estate can show (by submitting the appropriate documents from his mother's estate) that his interest was created by a third party (his mother).

Similarly, if mother had made a gift of the property to her three children as joint tenants, on the death of a child only one-third the value would be included in the deceased joint tenant's estate. As far as proof of the gift is concerned, the deed to the property would probably suffice. However, for property other than real estate—especially cash—proof of the gift could be a problem unless a gift tax return was filed.

SPECIAL RULE FOR HUSBAND AND WIFE

If the property is held by husband and wife under a tenancy by the entirety or under a joint tenancy with rights of survivorship (provided the husband and wife are the only joint tenants), then on the death of one, only *one-half* the value of the jointly held property will be included in the estate of the deceased joint owner regardless of who furnished the funds to purchase the property.

If a spouse (joint tenant) died before 1982, the rules were considerably more complicated, involving the consideration-furnished test described above, a "business participation" test, and a question of whether a gift was made. This has all been repealed, however, and the above "simple" rule applies for deaths after 1981.

The "simple" rule would work like this: James and Joanne have $800,000 of various types of property, all jointly held. On James's death, his estate tax return would show only $400,000 as his share of the jointly held property. With the new, unlimited marital deduction, however, it wouldn't matter whether it showed half the value, the full value, or three times the value. In other words, what may look like a break for spouses, has in fact turned out to be a *trap,* as shown below.

Trap Created by the Special Rule   When property is included in a person's estate for tax purposes, the estate tax is calculated on the fair value of that property on the date of the decedent's death (or as an alternative value, six months after death). The value used for estate tax purposes becomes the *beneficiary's new cost for income tax purposes*—this is referred to as the stepped-up cost basis.

For example, Sam buys some land as a speculation for $5,000 and takes title in joint names with his son, Steve. Several years later Sam dies and the land is then worth $80,000. Because Steve made no contribution, the full value of the jointly held land is included in Sam's estate and a small tax is paid. Steve now wants to sell the land at $80,000 and asks his tax advisor how much tax he'd have to pay on the gain. Answer: *None,* because Steve got a stepped-up cost basis equal to the value used for estate tax purposes—$80,000. It is treated just as if Steve *paid* $80,000 for the land. This would be the case even if there were no taxes in Sam's estate. Now let's see how this works for a surviving spouse.

Joseph purchases a summer home for $60,000 cash and takes title jointly with his wife, Catherine. Several years later Joseph dies, and the home is then worth $160,000. Because of the special rule discussed above, only one-half the value of the summer home ($80,000) will be included in Joseph's estate for tax purposes. The unlimited marital deduction, however, will render the $80,000 tax-free to Catherine, and she will get a stepped-up cost basis in *one-half* the property accordingly. But what about the other half? As to that half which was not included in Joseph's estate, she will retain the "old" cost basis of one-half the original price of $60,000 (or $30,000).

If she then sells the property for $160,000 the results will look like this (forgetting expenses):

Sales price	$160,000
less cost ¹/₂ (Joseph)	(80,000)
less cost ¹/₂ (Catherine)	(30,000)
Taxable *gain*	$ 50,000

If the full value of the property was included in Joseph's estate, there would still have been no estate tax and the capital gain (or potential gain) would have been eliminated.

What to do? Watch out for joint property! If it is highly appreciated and you don't plan on selling it before death, *get it out of joint!* (For some alternatives, see Chapters 13 and 14.) Of course the other side of that coin could provide a benefit, but considering statistics, it will be a rare case. That is, in the above example, if Catherine died before Joseph, then *he* would get a stepped-up cost basis in one-half the property (for which he paid a smaller amount). This possibility is not enough to run the risk of the reverse happening, unless, of course, there was a way of telling who would die first.

State Taxes   This discussion relates only to *federal* estate taxes. Don't forget that your state may take its share of estate taxes. Although a few states have no inheritance tax and others, such as Maryland and Oklahoma, do not tax property that passes to a surviving spouse, most states impose some form of estate tax (Nevada is the only state that has absolutely none) and this must be kept in mind when planning your estate. In fact, with the generous federal estate tax credits, most estates will pay a *state* estate tax but no *federal* estate tax.

D. ESTATE TAX SUMMARY

Perhaps the most misleading aspect about joint property insofar as it relates to estate taxes stems from the fact that it (probably) avoids probate, and the related but mistaken belief most people have that avoiding probate means avoiding estate taxes. Therefore, they hold joint property thinking that in avoiding probate it will avoid estate taxes. Forget it! One has nothing to do with the other.

Unless one of the exceptions to the general rule can be invoked, the *full value* of jointly held property is included in the estate of a deceased joint tenant. One exception allows the deceased joint tenant's estate to exclude the value attributable to the contribution of a surviving joint tenant (to the extent he can prove contribution), another allows an exclusion if the joint property was the subject of a gift or inheritance to the present joint tenants, in which case only the deceased joint tenant's fractional (equal) share will be included in his estate. Finally, only one-half the joint property held by husband and wife will be included in the estate of the first one to die regardless of contribution, but this is a deceiving benefit since it could lead to serious income tax problems for the surviving spouse.

Qualifying for any one of the exceptions generally requires some form of report or documentation with the IRS at the time the estate tax return is filed, so if there is any joint property in the estate the available exceptions must be reviewed to see if any applies.

4. PUTTING IT ALL TOGETHER

EXPOSURE TO THE VARIOUS gift, income, and estate tax aspects of joint property ought to convince even the most ardent of us that this simple form of ownership is not so simple after all. What's that you say? Joint ownership *is* simple, it's the tax laws that are complicated? Perhaps you're right. But breathing is simple too. It's the rest of the body that is complicated. And like joint property and taxes, it's tough to separate one from the other. Since they can't be separated, we'd better try to understand how they work best together.

We have seen that in many instances creation of a joint tenancy can result in a gift, the major exception to this being property held jointly by husband and wife. If and when a gift takes place, each joint tenant is taxed on his share of the income and this is so between husband and wife as well, but since they normally file a joint income tax return, it won't change the tax.

Another critical consideration is the very nature of the joint ownership, that is, the revered right of survivorship. From an estate tax standpoint it almost guarantees double taxation in the survivor's estate, and for this and many other reasons, joint property is a curse to the competent estate planner. On the death of the first joint owner, the full value of the property is included in the estate. Even if the marital deduction is allowed or some other exception applies, one-half the value is included. But then the survivor inherits the whole of the joint property and it is *all* taxed (again) in the survivor's estate. There are effective ways to avoid this, as suggested in Chapter 13.

11

JOINT TENANCY IN COMMUNITY PROPERTY STATES

INTRODUCTION AND WARNING

WHAT DO ARIZONA, CALIFORNIA, Idaho, Louisiana, Nevada, New Mexico, Texas, and Washington have in common? They are the only states out of our fifty which have adopted "community property" laws. In these states, the marital relationship is regarded as the "community," and property acquired during marriage often falls under the particular state's definition of community property.

The problem is that the community property laws of these eight states are not consistent from one state to the other, and so this brief chapter on community property as it relates to joint ownership (or vice versa) must be viewed as a general approach to the various considerations involved. Where a specific question or decision must be addressed, the laws of the applicable states must be reviewed.

1. BASICS OF COMMUNITY PROPERTY

COMMUNITY PROPERTY ITSELF is a form of co-tenancy very much like a tenancy in common. If spouses held property equally under a tenancy in common, each spouse would own an undivided one-half interest in the property and would be able to deal with it as his or her own, including having the right to partition the property to obtain his or her share. Similarly, when either spouse acquires what is considered to be community property, the law provides that each spouse has an undivided one-half interest in that property and this is so *regardless* of how title is held. That is, it could be in the husband's name alone, the wife's name alone, or even in both names, as we shall see.

In a community property state, community property is all property that is acquired by husband and wife while they have their principal residence in that state (and while married). There are, of course, exceptions to this general rule, and the two major exceptions that appear to apply in all the eight states are acquisition of property by gift and/or by inheritance.

For example, Elizabeth and Doug are married in Arizona in 1980 and during the next two years manage to save $10,000 through Doug's earnings. During that same period, Elizabeth's aunt dies and leaves her $25,000. The $10,000 they saved is community property and each has a right to one-half. The $25,000 inheritance is Elizabeth's *separate* property and Doug has no rights to it.

On the other hand, if Elizabeth's aunt left the $25,000 to Elizabeth *and* Doug, then the bequest would be their community property and each would have a one-half interest in the money (or whatever they buy with it). Similarly, if someone made a *gift* to Elizabeth, the gift would be her separate property, but if the gift were to *both* spouses (as a marriage gift), it would be community property.

In Idaho, Louisiana, and Texas, the *income* from a spouse's separate property is considered *community* property, while in the other five states, income from separate property is considered *separate* property. In the above example, if Elizabeth and Doug were domiciled in Idaho when she received the inheritance, then the income that is earned on the $25,000 (but not the $25,000 itself) is considered community property.

The obvious problem posed by community property versus separate property is keeping track of which is which. And the problem is particularly compounded when a couple who has acquired property (and who will acquire more) moves from a non-community property state into a community property state, or vice versa. Such problems are beyond the scope of this book, but when joint or other property is involved, the issues cannot be overlooked. Tracing the source of a couple's property can often be difficult and the lack of information can lead to tax and legal problems later. Therefore, it is a good practice to make and keep a running schedule of your property indicating what is believed to be community and what is not.

On the death of the spouse in a community property state, the community property is automatically divided so that one-half goes to the surviving spouse and the balance as directed in the will of the deceased spouse. In short, it is treated as if it were an equal tenancy in common. Questions can arise, though, where the community property is held in *both* names, purporting to be a joint tenancy with rights of survivorship. Whether it is or is not a joint tenancy and whether there will be rights of survivorship is not clear. It may depend upon the nature of the property, the actions of the parties, or even the particular state in which they live, as discussed below.

2. COMMUNITY PROPERTY AND JOINT TENANCY

A. SURVIVORSHIP RIGHTS

When married couples who reside in a community property state wish to acquire property in joint names so as to cause the survivor to receive the whole of the property, they may discover—too late—that they have a problem.

In most community property states the presumption is that *all* property acquired by the couple is community property, *regardless of how title is taken.* Therefore, what appears to be a joint tenancy may or may not be one, since the joint tenancy interest in some respects conflicts with the community property rights of a spouse. That is, each spouse has a right to dispose of his or her community property share during life or under a will without interference from the other. A joint tenancy, however, may operate to "pass" the deceased spouse's one-half interest to the survivor without regard to the previous deceased spouse's will—the two concepts are mutually exclusive. When there is a conflict in the will or when there are beneficiaries other than the surviving spouse, litigation can easily result.

Although all of the community property states recognize joint tenancies, they do not necessarily recognize joint tenancies between husband and wife when community property is involved. Texas, for example, has taken the position that it is unconstitutional for a married couple to create a joint tenancy out of community property. This would indicate that a husband or wife could transfer only his or her *separate* property into a joint tenancy between them. Even in the case of separate property, it is suggested that the couple have a written agreement outlining their intentions regarding the joint property. It should be noted that these rules apply only to husband and wife joint tenancies. Texas does recognize the right of spouses to transfer even community property to joint names with others. For example, a married couple may create a joint account with a child, even though the funds used were community funds. Further, it may be possible for husband and wife to *separate* their property and subsequently create a joint tenancy between them, but even this may be subject to question.

In California, on the other hand, a transfer of community property to joint tenancy between husband and wife is permitted, and creates the presumption that the parties intend to secure all the rights and responsibilities attendant to the joint tenancy, even though they differ in some respects from the community interest. Even in California, however, there can be no guarantee that a joint tenancy will operate to transfer the property to the surviving joint tenant if it can be shown that the couple did not intend to change the nature of their community interests.

Agreements May Help

Because of the potential conflicts between the community interest and the survivorship interests, couples who wish to create a joint tenancy with community property should consider written agreements clearly describing their intentions with respect to the joint property and the survivorship rights. Such agreements should not be arbitrarily done, since they could affect other marital rights and in some states may have no more than evidentiary value. Without an agreement, however, there would be *no basis* for proving that the parties intended to give up their respective community interests in the property, and even a casual attack by an heir could destroy the survivorship interests.

It appears that all the community property states except Texas and Louisiana recognize the right of a couple to enter an agreement after the marriage specifying the character of their assets. But even in Texas and Louisiana it would appear that a written agreement properly executed by the parties would be given evidentiary value in the event the *intention* of the parties was the issue.

Tenancy in Common

The community property interest is almost identical to the tenancy in common in the respect that each spouse (or tenant) has an undivided interest—in this case, one-half—in the whole of the property, and may dispose of that interest without interference from the other spouse (or tenant). The only apparent distinction is that a tenancy in common will usually disclose the names of the tenants on the title to the property, whereas a community property interest may be in the name of the husband only or the wife only, or both. Given these characteristics and the fact that there is no survivorship interest in the tenancy in common, this form of ownership does not present a serious problem in community property states.

B. CREDITOR'S RIGHTS—JOINT PROPERTY

Whether the community property has become a bona fide joint interest may make a difference where creditors are concerned. As a general rule, all the community property states except California recognize what are called "community debts." These are all debts incurred by the spouses while married, based on the presumption that such debts are for the benefit of the "community" or marriage, unless it can clearly be proved otherwise. Once a debt is determined to be a community debt, a creditor can satisfy his claim out of community property.

There are, of course, exceptions to this rule and the laws vary from state to state. For example, some states do not allow a creditor to reach the community property for a husband's individual debts, while others do. And most states (of the eight involved) do not allow a creditor to reach the community property for a wife's individual debts, except for "necessities" or where she was acting as her husband's agent.

Insofar as all this applies to joint tenancies, if the community property is held to be a valid joint tenancy, then it may be that a creditor (of one of the spouses), who would otherwise be able to reach the entire community property in question, would be able to reach only one-half the jointly held property. This possibility of "protecting" one-half the joint property should *by no means* be considered reason to convert any part of your community property to a joint tenancy, as there are many other factors and consequences to consider, most of them offering unfavorable complications. Therefore, the question of exposure to creditors may be more academic then practical from a planning standpoint.

C. SEPARATING PROPERTY TO FORM JOINT TENANCY

It is permissible for a couple to separate their community property so that each is left with his or her share of the community property. Although there may be tax or legal implications to such a division, and it would not apply to subsequently acquired property, each would then have his and her individual property and would be able to create joint or other interests with that separate property as he or she saw fit.

This type of move is somewhat drastic merely to effect a transfer to joint names (which in itself can present tax and legal problems) and should not be considered without the approval of competent counsel.

SUMMARY

COMMUNITY PROPERTY RIGHTS, recognized in Arizona, California, Idaho, Louisiana, Nevada, New Mexico, Texas, and Washington, give each spouse an equal interest in all property acquired during marriage regardless of whether the property is in the husband's name, the wife's name, or both. This underlying presumption can present problems when the spouses attempt to change their interests by creating a joint tenancy with rights of survivorship. Because the community property laws are not consistent from state to state, some (such as California) may recognize the joint tenancy while others (such as Texas) may not.

Where property is gifted to the spouses or inherited by them under the specific provision that they take as joint tenants with rights of survivorship, it may be that the joint tenancy is recognized, but the result could vary depending upon the state. Where property is gifted or inherited by one of the spouses it becomes her or his separate property and may subsequently be transferred to joint names if desired, but there are other tax and legal factors to consider.

Even in those states that allow a transfer of community property to joint names, a written agreement between the spouses is advisable, outlining their intentions relating to the survivorship interest and their community property shares. Obviously, in those states where there is a question as to the allowability of a transfer to joint names, a written agreement, properly signed, is a *must* if there is to be any hope of maintaining the joint tenancy.

Finally, and most importantly, the discussions in this chapter of transferring property from community to joint is designed to address objectively the issue of whether such a transfer is either advisable or desirable, since a thorough reading of this book should indicate that on the whole it is *not*.

CHAPTER

12

AVOIDING PROBATE
THROUGH JOINT TENANCY
AND OTHER BAD IDEAS

INTRODUCTION

GREEK MYTHOLOGY TELLS US that sailors always had to be on their guard against sirens—beautiful women whose irresistible songs lured the sailors into perilous waters. The sailors were continually warned that the women and their songs were nothing more than illusions, but in spite of the warnings, the sailors just could not resist the attraction. Joint ownership has its own siren song, and despite the warnings, we continue to use it more than any other form of ownership.

The sweet song of survivorship and avoiding probate and taxes makes joint ownership practically irresistible, even though it is largely a siren's song. We have seen, for example, that instead of avoiding taxes, joint ownership of property can increase taxes, and we have seen that the promise of avoiding probate can be nothing more than an illusion. It might happen, but then again it might not. Actually, the promise of avoiding probate through joint ownership is quite a fragile one. The executor or administrator of an estate or a disgruntled heir or even a creditor can

171

interfere with the survivorship interest with ease. How? Through the probate process itself. A brief explanation of this process might help you understand why you may want to avoid it and, later, how.

1. WHAT IS PROBATE?

IT COMES AS A SURPRISE TO many people that we have no inherent *right* to leave our property to others after our death. The rights we do have in this respect are given to us by statutes or state laws. Every state has a law allowing a person "of sound mind and over the age of majority" to dispose of his property by a will. Of course, there is a corresponding law in each state telling us who will inherit our property if we *don't* have a will—generally called the law of "descent and distribution."

When a person dies owning any property at all, someone must be responsible for seeing to it that the deceased person's property passes according to his will, or according to the laws of the state if he left no will. But what if he left several wills (like Howard Hughes), or what if there is a question whether the will is valid or whether he forgot to include a certain family member. And what about his debts. Should they be paid out of his estate?

Finally, how does the property legally get from the deceased's name to the name of the beneficiary? Someone must see to these issues as well, and that someone is the probate court.

The Probate Court—in some states the Orphan's Court, Surrogate Court, or Chancery Court—is responsible for overseeing the probate procedure. The court seldom takes action on its own. If someone dies and no one ever applies to the probate court for probate proceedings in that estate, no probate will result.

Without (at this point) addressing the question of whether probate should or should not be avoided, it is a fact that in many cases, such as the ones raised above, probate is a necessary process. If a person dies with property in his own name, it is *only* through the probate procedure that anyone can legally receive this property. It is not difficult to visualize the chaos and "looting" that would result if people were allowed to simply *take* the property of a deceased person without regard to the claims of anyone else. It makes sense, then, to have an official arbiter for *all* the questions that arise after a person's death.

The probate system provides that function. It offers a systematic way of settling claims and *transferring property* after a person's death. However, the probate court has jurisdiction only over *probate property*. Basically, this is property that was in the deceased's name *alone* at the time of his death. The probate court will satisfy itself that the deceased's last will is valid and will then see to it that the probate property passes according to the will or according to the laws of the state if there was no valid will. This is done, of course, after payment of allowable debts and expenses.

This entire procedure—a procedure fully open to the eyes of an inquisitive public—functions primarily to transfer property from the deceased to others. And since it is potentially time-consuming and involved, attorney's fees can be formidable. So why not, you may ask, try to avoid probate if you can? Maybe you should. But there are different ways of doing this—some wiser than others. Further, depending upon the size of your estate, some postmortem tax-planning benefits could be lost if probate is totally avoided. Nevertheless, in my opinion the avoidance of probate, *if properly done,* can eliminate considerable fees, delays, contests, exposure, and publicity on a person's death. But *only* if properly done. A do-it-yourself attempt at it that fails could easily produce a result far worse than if the entire estate were passed through the probate system.

2. WAYS OF AVOIDING PROBATE

THERE ARE FOUR WAYS OF transferring property at death. Only one is through probate. The other three are the result of some disposition or arrangement made by the deceased *during his life* but designed to effect a transfer at death. For example, one would be a contractual arrangement in which the performance or promise of the other party involves payment of funds to beneficiaries of the deceased after his death. A life insurance policy is an illustration of this: the owner pays the premiums and the insurance company agrees to pay the death proceeds to a named beneficiary. By naming a beneficiary, the property (cash proceeds of the policy) is effectively transferred without the need of the probate process. That is, the money is paid directly to the beneficiary without passing through probate. But if the named beneficiary is the "estate of the insured," then the proceeds will not only be fully probated but will be fully taxable as well. For this and other reasons, insurance policies should almost never be made payable to your estate.

Another illustration would be certain company benefits that are paid after the employee's death under the agreement or contract he had with his employer. For example, a contract might provide that on an employee's death his spouse will receive $5,000 per year for five years. These amounts paid *directly* to the spouse (or other beneficiary) do not pass through probate, since there was a contractual agreement to pay them to a specific person or persons after death.

The two remaining and perhaps most popular means of transferring property at death without passing through probate are *trusts* and *joint ownership.*

If the deceased had transferred property to a trust during his life with instructions as to the disposition of that property after his death, there would be no need to engage the probate court to effect a transfer. His lifetime disposition (or transfer) has already taken care of that. For example, if Bill gives a painting to Sandy and asks her to "hold" it "in trust" until his death, at which time Sandy may give it to their daughter Sally, then on Bill's death, Sandy may immediately deliver the securities to Sally without interference or permission of the probate court. This is on account of Bill's *lifetime* transfer of the securities into a trust, with instructions for disposition after his death. In a sense, the painting did not belong to him at his death—it was already disposed of through the trust and there was no need for the probate court to participate in a transfer. (Trusts are discussed in detail in the next chapter.)

Joint ownership is the fourth way to transfer property at death, although it ranks first in popularity, without justification. The basic understanding of a joint tenancy between two owners is that on the death of one, the survivor automatically owns the whole of the jointly held property. It is thought of as a sort of inheritance.

From a legal standpoint, a valid joint tenancy is the result of a lifetime transfer, which "vests" or becomes the property of each succeeding survivor by "operation of law." In other words, the property really *already* belonged to the survivor, subject only to the claim of the other joint tenant. It is *not* inherited. When a joint tenant dies, his interest and any claim he might have held disappears, so the property, which belonged to the survivor subject to that claim, is now the survivor's free and clear of any claim. A transfer of ownership that automatically takes place by "operation of law" needs no outside action or verification by probate courts, lawyers, deeds, or the like. It can be quite a smooth transition from one tenant to another. That is, of course, if there are no objections. Unfortunately, where money and emotions are concerned, things don't always work the way they are supposed to.

If you haven't already guessed by reading some of the cases in the preceding chapters, joint tenancies enjoy as much popularity *in* the courts as they do outside because they are treated in such an arbitrary fashion by the creators of the joint tenancies. This in turn makes them quite vulnerable to attack.

Using joint tenancies to avoid probate can be extremely risky. It not only invites litigation when there is the slightest question of intent, but (depending on the size of the estate) it can produce extra taxes and even extra administrative (probate) fees—the very thing it was thought to prevent! These points have been clearly illustrated over and over in previous chapters by actual cases showing the disputes that can arise and the costs and delays involved.

In addition to intentional interference with the survivorship interest, it may be that a *lack* of interference can also result in upsetting an estate plan. In Chapter 7, for example, we discussed convenience bank accounts, where a joint tenant was added for convenience rather than with the intent that he or she receive the money on death. If the contributing tenant dies and no objections are raised, the surviving joint tenant will end up with the proceeds, even though it was the deceased's intention that they go to someone else, and it is not likely that the surviving tenant will volunteer to pay the money back.

Another risk is the possibility of simultaneous death of the joint owners. This was discussed much earlier in the book, but basically it has the effect of converting the joint tenancy into a tenancy in common. This would result in one-half the property passing through the *probate* estate of *each joint tenant,* and would bring about extra fees, delays, and taxes, unless the will or trust of one of the joint tenants contains a provision dealing with simultaneous death.

And even if the joint property succeeds in passing to the survivor on the death of a joint tenant, there is still the problem of the property being probated in the estate of the survivor, who is then the sole owner. To hope that the survivor will create some new joint tenancies in the future is merely to defer the risk of the same tax and legal problems to a later date, not to mention the fact that the original owner (and each succeeding owner) will have completely lost control of the funds after his death and the right to dispose of them as well. Joint ownership, unless attacked, can override the provisions of a will.

Because the property in a joint tenancy belongs to the survivor by operation of law, i.e., automatically, the provisions of a will have no bearing on the dispositions of the jointly held property, unless, as previously discussed, someone attacks the validity of the joint tenancy. This loss of the right to dispose of your property should not be treated lightly or overlooked, since it is the conflicting dispositions of property between the joint tenancy and the will that cause the most problems. For example, say that a mother has most of her money in a joint account with her daughter. In her will she leaves everything to her *three* children equally. Chances are that the mother thought this included her joint account with her daughter. Further chances are that the other two children will ask the daughter to "divvy" up the joint account proceeds since this is what the mother intended. Probably her daughter will find some good reasons to justify keeping all the money left in the joint account. Solution? Most likely a cash settlement after protracted litigation and payment of probate and legal fees.

If the mother had thought of this potential problem and had not one but *three* joint accounts in roughly equal amounts with a different child as a co-tenant on each account, each child (if no one objected) would have taken the proceeds in her or his respective joint account without the need for probate in the mother's estate. Of course, this does not take into account the rest of the mother's property, nor does it consider the death of a child prior to the mother's. More problems.

In short, it may happen that joint property will avoid probate, but the risks that it will not, and that even if it does it will produce other problems and concerns, far outweigh the possible benefits.

A possible and important exception might occur when the home—the principal residence—is held jointly (or under a tenancy by the entirety) by husband and wife. Seldom are there objections or interferences with the surviving spouse taking this property on the death of the other. Therefore, unless some other type of ownership is recommended by advisors, married couples owning their home jointly need not rush out to change the title. Similarly, a bank account or money market account of "nominal" size in joint names of husband and wife is helpful for quick access to funds on death or disability of the other. By nominal size I mean an amount sufficient to meet emergency needs in the context of your family's lifestyle. For some families it may be $1,000, for other $20,000. You must decide for yourself.

These exceptions for husband and wife where the home and a small bank account are concerned are somewhat of a concession on my part. Many of the risks—simultaneous death, permanent disability, divorce—are still present. Nevertheless, I feel that in the case of the home and emergency funds, the risks are "calculated" ones and if the rest of the estate plan is in order, they are in effect minimized.

ANOTHER BAD IDEA

IF YOU RECOGNIZE THAT JOINT ownership can create problems, you must then consider the alternative ways to transfer your property at death. One is to keep all your property in your own name and pass it by way of your will. Assuming you have a properly drafted will, the chances of interference with this disposition of your property are greatly reduced. The only problem is that your entire estate passes through probate, and with it the attendant fees, delays, exposure to claims, and publicity. In other words, this is for the most part (and in my opinion) a bad idea. But you have another alternative for transferring your property at death and avoiding probate to boot. A trust.

Trusts—living trusts—allow you to keep full control of your property while you're alive and well, and then to pass the property on to named beneficiaries after your death without the need for probate. In the meantime, a trust can offer additional benefits and protection, as well as certain tax benefits after your death. What they are, how to do it, and what choices you have are discussed in detail in Chapter 13.

SUMMARY

IN CERTAIN CASES THE probate process is necessary, but in general, it makes sense to avoid it. Passing all your property under a will and therefore through probate is probably the more expensive way to pass property. Although a major temptation of joint ownership is the suggestion that it will avoid probate on your death, don't fall for it. The risks of additional probate costs through an attack on the joint tenancies and the risks of upsetting your estate and tax plans make the joint tenancy choice a bad one. Possible exceptions are considered for married couples where the home and an emergency bank account are concerned, but even here the risks must be respected.

Other means of avoiding probate include life insurance or other "contractual" arrangements (such as employee benefits), and finally, *living trusts,* which, in my opinion, are the best way.

13

TRUSTS—A CURE FOR THE JOINT PROPERTY ADDICT

INTRODUCTION

ADDICTION: "AN HABITUAL dependency on something without regard to its effect." Does this describe your approach to joint ownership? Isn't it true that you often automatically resort to this type of ownership without fully knowing the effects it may have on you or your family? You have undoubtedly learned by now that it can prove to be an expensive habit.

Fortunately, there is a cure for the habit. It's called a trust. A trust (a "living" trust) can offer you *all the advantages of joint ownership with none of the disadvantages*. It can provide for survivorship interest, it can allow easy access to property, such as bank accounts, in case of illness or death, and it can cause property to avoid probate. Further, as will be seen in this chapter, it can also be designed to do many other things, far beyond the capacity of a joint tenancy.

But there are many different forms of trusts, and the different trusts may contain different provisions. Some may do the job while others will not. You must be careful that your trust accomplishes your wishes and will do the job for you. To understand this you should know a little about trusts, what they are and how they work.

1. BASICS OF TRUSTS

THE FUNDAMENTAL TRUST arrangement involves a transfer of property to someone on his promise that he will hold it for another. It is a unique and useful relationship that clearly reflects its very name—a *trust*. However, like many legal principles and relationships, the modern-day trust has evolved to embody the latest legal and tax developments in many different areas. Nevertheless, the basics remain the same, and if you understand these you will understand how a trust can help you.

According to some experts the concept of the trust traces back nearly two thousand years to the reign of Emperor Augustus Caesar. At that time a Roman citizen and his wife, who was not of the Roman Empire, wanted to leave their property to their children, but under Roman law the children were not allowed to inherit because their mother was not a Roman. To circumvent this law, the Roman left his property through his will to a friend, also a Roman, on his friend's promise that he would use the property to provide for the Roman's children after the Roman's death.

In this case, the friend betrayed the trust that the Roman had placed in him and used the property for himself. The Emperor Augustus, shocked at the betrayal, referred the matter to the Roman court for disposition. Prior to this, the use of such a bequest (*in trust*) had never been formally recognized by the court, but after the Emperor's approval the arrangement became so popular that a special court had to be established to answer inquiries and determine the treatment of such cases.

This was one of the earliest recorded forms of trust, but it contains all the basic ingredients of today's trusts. The Roman (called the *donor* or the *grantor* or the *settlor*) transferred property (sometimes called the *corpus*) to his friend (called the *trustee*) who promised to follow instructions to hold and use the property for the benefit of the children (the *beneficiaries*).

From its simplest form to the most complex, every trust is based upon the same principle and contains the same basic elements: a donor, a trustee, some property, and one or more beneficiaries.

2. THE LIVING TRUST

A LIVING TRUST IS ANY TRUST that you create while you are alive. It is sometimes referred to as an "inter vivos" trust—meaning, among the living. The opposite of a living trust is a *testamentary* trust.

The trust created by our Roman was a testamentary trust—that is, it was created *at his death* by instructions contained in his will. In order for the trust to take effect, then, the Roman's will had to be approved by a court, and this is only done through the probate process. If the Roman had created a *living* trust and had transferred his property to the trust during his lifetime with instructions for its disposition after his death, there would have been no need for the probate court to make the transfer. The property already *in* the trust would have avoided the probate process.

Under most living trusts, the creator or donor will reserve the right to "alter, amend, or revoke" the trust. This simply means he can do whatever he pleases with the trust or with any property held in the trust. The retention of a right to change or revoke the trust—called a *revocable* trust—does not provide the donor with any immediate tax benefits but will allow the property in the trust to avoid the costs, delays, and publicity of probate.

The opposite of a revocable trust is an *irrevocable* trust. If a trust does not specifically contain the right to amend or revoke, it is automatically irrevocable—it generally *cannot* be changed. Although current tax savings can be realized through the use of an irrevocable trust, you should consider one *only* after proper advice and counsel, since the document is relatively permanent and recovery of the property transferred to such a trust is unlikely.

3. HOW A TRUST WORKS

WHETHER YOUR TRUST IS living or testamentary, whether it is revocable or irrevocable, or whether it is a simple "trustee" bank account or a complicated family trust, once it takes effect it will work the same way.

When property is transferred to the trustee, the trustee immediately begins to manage, maintain, or invest the property, whether it be cash, securities, real estate, or other property, according to the instructions given by the donor. For example, say that John gives $1,000 to Mary with instructions that she give him (John) all the interest it earns, then on John's death, she should turn the balance over to his sister Adele. Mary's duties are quite clear. She will pay John all the interest up to the time of his death, then transfer the funds over to Adele, directly. Adele then owns the money outright and Mary's job as trustee is completed.

Of course, the instructions and/or the duties could be much more involved. John could have transferred real estate to Mary, or a large portfolio of various securities, and Mary would be responsible for the proper management of the trust property. This might include renting the property, keeping it properly insured and in good repair, and so on. If she were holding securities, she would be responsible for keeping track of the progress of the various companies whose stock she was holding or she might simply hire an investment advisor. But in any event, once the property is transferred to the trust, the trustee's responsibility is to care for it while carrying out the donor's instructions to her.

4. WHAT CAN A TRUST DO?

THE TRUST INSTRUMENT IS ONE of the most flexible legal tools available today. Rather than enumerate all that it can do, its flexibility is better understood by stating what it cannot do—it cannot be created to do anything that is illegal or against public policy. Anything else is permissible. For example, a trust can:

run a business
provide for minors or elderly persons
pay medical or other bills
create a scholarship fund
provide for retirement, education, marriage, and even divorce
hold real estate, cash, securities, or any other type of property
avoid probate and some administrative costs for property in the
     trust
  provide protection for property in trust against creditors of the
     beneficiaries

Our Roman citizen established a trust to care for his children. Simple enough, but also one of the essential reasons for a trust. The Roman must have been a wise person. Even in the year A.D. 5 he knew that a youth and his money are soon parted, and that it may be better to allow his children only the *use* of the property until they reached an age of greater maturity, when they might better appreciate the value of money and the responsibility that goes with it.

Your reasons for creating a trust may be some, all, or none of the above. Or it may be just to avoid probate. Whatever the reasons, your trust can be specially tailored to accomplish your objectives, leaving little to chance. In light of this it is foolhardy to rely upon the whimsical joint ownership form to dispose of your property when a simple trust can accomplish the same thing and more.

5. FUNDING YOUR TRUST

SOME OF YOU READING THIS may feel complacent in that you already have a trust. If this is so, congratulations—maybe! Set aside your complacency for the moment to see if your trust has been "funded." A trust is funded when property is transferred to it. Your trust will operate or have effect only as to *that* property that has been actually transferred to the trust.

Perhaps the most common estate planning mistake is having a trust, then failing to fund it. By funding I do not mean a transfer of $10 or $100 or by naming the trust as beneficiary of your life insurance policy. I mean funding it with just about *all* of your property. Depending upon the state in which you live, you may need a different trust to hold your real estate, but this can easily be drafted to coordinate with the terms of any other trust (or trusts) you have.

The big mistake is going to the trouble of having a trust, but continuing to hold most of your property in joint names. The jointly held property will, unless someone objects, pass to the surviving joint tenant and *not* to your trust. As to this property, then, your trust becomes worthless.

I recently had a case in which a father went to a great deal of trouble to create a trust for his retarded daughter. It was an elaborate, well-drafted trust, which provided for the daughter's care for the rest of her life since she was unable to care for herself. On the father's death, his widow came to me to determine the next step so that the trust could begin to provide for the child. An examination of the father's assets disclosed that everything he owned was in joint names with his wife. *Nothing* passed to the daughter's trust!

In the more common situation, the husband will have a marital and a family trust to accomplish his estate and tax planning, but most of his property, being jointly held, will pass outside the trust, rendering the trust useless and frustrating the estate plan.

Funding your trust, then, to the maximum practical extent possible will allow you to get the benefits intended by the trust, during life as well as after death. One of the important lifetime benefits is realized if you become disabled. If jointly held securities or real estate is involved, at least one-half the value of the joint property would be "frozen," and in any event a sale would not be allowed until the probate court appointed a guardian or conservator for you. If instead you had placed this property in a trust, *no* court action would be required. The property would be immediately accessible by the trustee to provide for your care and treatment. This can be extremely important in the case of a widow or widower or other single person.

Exactly how to fund your trust and the tax and legal implications of this are discussed in Chapter 14.

6. WHO SHOULD BE TRUSTEE

IF YOU FUND YOUR TRUST WHILE you are alive, you should usually be your own trustee. It is quite permissible for you to be donor, trustee, and beneficiary all at the same time, *provided* your trust provides for some other beneficiary (or beneficiaries) after your death. Naming yourself as initial trustee allows you to maintain *full control* over your property as long as you wish and are able. In the event of your death or disability, your trust would provide for a "successor" trustee, who would take over that position for you and administer the trust property for your and your family's benefit.

The successor trustee is guided (and restricted) by the terms of your trust. He cannot use the funds for his own benefit or go against your instructions. If he does, he will be *personally responsible* for his breach of "fiduciary" duty—the duty of a trustee to always act in the best interests of the beneficiaries and in accordance with the terms of the trust.

Although naming yourself as a trustee is an easy choice, selecting a successor trustee is often not so easy. The successor trustee in many trusts must usually be an independent one for tax purposes. Therefore, a spouse or child may not qualify. And even if they do, a good deal of thought should be given to placing such a burden on them.

Our Roman citizen named his friend as trustee and it turned out to be a poor choice. His friend had no experience in such matters and proved to be untrustworthy. In those days, perhaps there were few people who could have had much experience, but a more reliable person may have at least carried out the donor's wishes.

Being a trustee may be easy if you are also the donor and beneficiary. You can do with the property as you please and you have only yourself to answer to. If you become a trustee where someone else is the beneficiary, you're in a whole new ball game. Everything you do is subject to review and question by the beneficiaries. Investments, distributions, timing of both, selling, buying, leasing, preparing and filing tax returns and trust accounts, all must be done with your fiduciary duty in mind, otherwise you could find yourself covering mistakes with your own money! People who really understand the serious responsibility and duties involved usually do not wish to act as trustee for someone else, unless they have considerable experience—and the time to do it. As a result, more and more people are relying on those organizations that have the experience and the time to give the trust the necessary attention. They are called corporate trustees.

A corporate trustee is a bank or trust company chartered by the state to accept funds from members of the public under a trust agreement. Although there may be something to be said against corporate trustees, there are a good many important points in their favor. Most corporate trustees have been in the trust business for years and know how to manage a trust. They have a reputation to uphold and so do not want bad press if they can avoid it. They have financial backing and stability so the chances of their running off with your money are slim, if not nonexistent. Their fees are regulated by law or by the probate court and are usually disclosed to you before you name them as trustee.

"On the other hand," as we lawyers are wont to say, corporate trustees have been accused of being cold and unresponsive to the members of the family, and have been known to be somewhat stiff and inflexible when it comes to interpretation of the trust provisions. In addition, they are not known for their outstanding investment performance. All of these "other-handed" objections, however, can be dealt with by adding two provisions to your trust: first, have your spouse or another family member act as *co-trustee* with the bank. This will add the warmth and sensitivity that may be lacking in a bank. Second, give your spouse (or other responsible family member or members) the right to *remove* the corporate trustee and appoint a successor (corporate or disinterested) trustee.

Granted, the power to remove can be abused and in the wrong hands it can jeopardize the proper administration of the trust. But you'll just have to trust someone.

7. THE TERMS OF YOUR TRUST

IF YOU ARE GOING TO THE trouble of having a trust, go one step further and be sure it has terms that the trustee can follow and that properly reflect your wishes—otherwise it may be a waste of your time. The lazy man's trust, the trustee bank account, for example, is little better than a joint account. The trustee bank account is a trust that in effect has no terms other than the trustee's absolute right to make deposits and withdrawals as he sees fit, and the right of the beneficiary (subject to easy interference) to receive the funds on the trustee's death.

In order for the terms of a trust to be carried out, there have to be some terms. Where there are none or where the terms are incomplete or contradictory or confusing, there will be trouble with a capital T, and that rhymes with P and you know the rest.

The terms may be simple or they may be complicated but they must be clear. They should cover lifetime distributions of income and/or principal, the conditions or guidelines for distributions, and the possibility that a beneficiary may die before the donor or before receiving his or her distributions. There should be provisions for successor trustees and for adequate trustee powers, as well as protection of the funds from claims of creditors (called a "spendthrift" provision), to name only a few. Attorneys experienced in drafting trusts are well versed in the numerous provisions that can and should be included.

A final word about the terms of your trust. *Don't be conned* into using preprinted forms. As pointed out a little later, the only person who benefits from these forms is the person who sells them to you.

8. USING A TRUST TO SAVE ESTATE TAXES

IF ALL OR THE MAJORITY OF your property is jointly owned with your spouse or with another person, it will be subject to estate taxes twice—once on your death, then again on the death of the survivor. Depending upon the size of your estate and the time of death this arrangement is literally like throwing money away. For example, an $800,000 estate all jointly held with a surviving spouse will pay an *extra* federal estate tax of over $75,000 (on the death of both spouses) even though both deaths occur after 1987 when the maximum estate tax credit goes into effect. If one death occurred *before* that, the extra tax could be even more! And if the surviving joint owner is not a spouse, the tax loss is even greater. All for the convenience of avoiding probate!

Through the use of a living trust, the double tax created in these situations can be *completely eliminated* while still realizing the desired objective of avoiding probate.

The way taxes are saved through a trust is by having the property "bypass" the estate of the beneficiary, so that it escapes the second tax. This can be done even though the beneficiary has the right to *use and enjoy* the property in the trust. A very typical and effective estate plan for a married couple with children uses this approach in the form of so-called "A and B" trusts, or the marital trust (the "A" trust) and the family trust (the "B" trust).

The *marital trust* is designed to take advantage of the marital deduction allowed under federal law. Being a deduction from the taxable estate, the marital deduction may pass to the spouse (or to a trust for the spouse) free of any federal estate tax. Beginning in 1982, the amount that may pass tax-free to a surviving spouse is unlimited. This does not mean, however, that everything should therefore be left to the surviving spouse. To do so will produce extra federal taxes if the deceased husband's estate exceeds $600,000, because the opportunity of utilizing any allowable tax credit will be lost.

For example, Grant dies in 1987 with an estate of $800,000 and leaves it all to his wife, Grace. There will be no tax on Grant's death because of the unlimited marital deduction. However, Grant's estate lost the opportunity to use his $600,000 exemption because the marital deduction on the full estate eliminated any further tax considerations. The problem is, on Grace's subsequent death, her estate will be allowed only the $600,000 exemption equivalent, and the tax on the remaining $200,000 will be about $75,000.

If Grant had instead left Grace everything *over* the allowable exemption (of $600,000), then there would be no tax on Grant's death and no tax on Grace's death—a savings of $75,000.

This could be done by leaving your spouse a "formula" amount tied in to the allowable exemption. Your spouse's share under this formula could be left in a trust (the marital trust or "A" trust) under her control for her life. With the property held in trust, it would avoid exposure to the probate court on her disability or death. The balance of the estate (an amount equal to the allowable tax-free exemption) would be held in a family trust (the "B" trust), which may be operated for the benefit of the spouse and/or other members of the family, or anyone else the donor wants to benefit. Typically, however, it operates for the spouse and children, and continues for the rest of the spouse's life. Since she does not *own* the property in this family trust, it is not included in her estate and therefore *not taxed* on her subsequent death.

Under the usual arrangement where the family trust provides for the spouse for her life, then for the children until they reach a certain age, say thirty, there is *no tax* on the spouse's death and *no tax* when the children receive distribution at age thirty. At one time it was even possible to bypass the children's estates, so the property could pass *untaxed* to grandchildren and even great grandchildren, skipping the successive generations. This was how the rich used to do it. In 1976 Congress passed a law imposing a "generation-skipping" tax, which in effect put the kibosh on generation-skipping trusts. However, one small break was left available. There is an "exemption" from the tax of up to $250,000 per child of the donor.

This exemption would allow a parent with three children, for example, to establish a trust of up to $750,000 (3 × $250,000) and provide benefits for his spouse for her life, then his children *for their lives,* then over to his grandchildren at a predetermined age. In this case, there would be *no tax* on the trust on the spouse's death, *no tax* on the children's death, and *no tax* when the grandchildren receive the funds, all the while avoiding probate and estate administrative expenses. Beats the daylights out of joint property.

9. USING PREPRINTED, TEAR-OUT FORMS—
A DONATION TO YOUR LOCAL LAWYER

JUST A WORD ABOUT THE USE OF preprinted forms of trusts. You ought to approach these in the same way you would a cheap suit of clothes bought from a mail-order supply house. The price may be right but you'd be a fool to think it will fit or be fit to wear. So it is with forms.

In a recent unjustifiably popular book on avoiding probate there is a myriad of trust forms, with step-by-step instructions on their use. The instructions, however, fail to take into consideration any gift or other tax results (in fact, following the instructions will often result in *additional* taxes). In addition, they fail to consider the possible conflicts from one form to another when compared with your overall estate plan; they fail to adequately consider death or disability of your beneficiaries; they completely overlook coordination from one form to another; and *most dangerously,* they encourage you to go merrily along arbitrarily filling in the blanks, without knowing the slightest thing about what you are doing. And for what? For a savings of maybe a few hundred dollars in legal fees, since the *last* thing you should do—such books tell us—is consult a lawyer. The unguided use of such forms might result in avoidance of probate with some of your property, but it will more likely result in *added fees* for court interpretation of conflicting documents, *added taxes,* and *added costs* in the estates of the beneficiaries. You might as well have spent your money on a cheap suit.

When you think of the tens of thousands of dollars in savings that can definitely—not maybe, as with uncoordinated forms—be saved through the use of a professionally drafted *and funded* trust, properly coordinated with the rest of your estate plan, it is silly and reckless to try to do-it-yourself with the help of forms you know nothing about prepared by some would-be lawyer.

10. HOW TO START YOUR TRUST

THE VERY BEST WAY TO BEGIN serious consideration of your own trust is by doing exactly what you are doing now—reading about it. There is plenty of material available at libraries, banks, and bookstores. Do not try to become an expert but do try to develop a good understanding of what you and your trust can and cannot do. Once you have some familiarity with the trust concept, call your attorney and ask him how familiar he is with funded, inter-vivos (living) trusts and whether he can develop an estate plan for you that is designed to avoid probate. Be frank and direct in your questions. If he (or she) gets overly defensive, he is probably not familiar enough with the area, and you should look around for another attorney.

Most bar associations have lawyer referral services, and they should be able to give you the names of two or three local attorneys who have indicated a familiarity with tax and estate planning. And don't be afraid to call these (or other) attorneys to request an initial conference—preferably a free one. Many attorneys are willing to give you fifteen minutes or a half hour without charge to determine whether they can help you and to see if the "chemistry" is right.

Once you have selected and met with an attorney and your estate plan is developed and ready to go, stop where you are. At this point you should spend $100 or so and get a second opinion on the plan that has been presented to you. The second opinion may be that of another attorney or your accountant or even your bank's trust department (an advantage here is that the bank and the bank's trust attorney will not usually charge you for their reveiw). If the opinion is favorable, you may proceed with the plan. If not, the issues raised may be discussed and resolved with your attorney, and your final plan may then be implemented.

Part of your plan will undoubtedly involve funding or transferring property to your trust. (If it doesn't, you probably don't have the right plan.) This is the legal move which actually starts your trust. As previously discussed, once the trust is funded, it then takes effect. It is a *disposition* of the property, and the property will from that point on be administered and distributed according to the terms of your trust because it is *in* the trust, even though you may be the trustee. Your attorney, banker, accountant, insurance advisor, and stockbroker may each play a part in the important steps required to fund your trust, as discussed in the next chapter.

CHAPTER

14

WHAT TO DO WITH YOUR JOINT PROPERTY NOW

BY NOW IT SHOULD BE CLEAR that we must approach all forms of co-tenancies with caution and with at least a basic understanding of what we may be in for. We have seen, for instance, that a joint tenancy may or may not pass to the survivor, depending upon the intent of the parties, the nature of the property, and whether anyone wishes to object to its passing to the survivor. There are numerous cases illustrating a variety of endings to the same fact patterns. We have also seen that the relationship of the joint tenants to one another can make a difference in the outcome of a case. There are, for example, certain presumptions when husband and wife are the co-tenants, and the parent/child joint tenancy would appear to be much more defensible than that where a deceased and his lawyer were the joint tenants.

If you become involved in any type of co-tenancy, be sure that you are clear in your understanding of your rights as to that property. Often a tenancy in common is thought to be a joint tenancy just because two people are co-owners of the property. There is, as you know, a major distinction between these two types of ownership—the joint tenancy can carry rights of survivorship while the tenancy in common does *not*. The share of a deceased tenant in common passes through his probate estate. So check the deed or other document creating the co-tenancy to determine the type of co-tenancy you have. If the document does not state whether it is joint tenants or as tenants in common, it may be either, depending upon your state law and the relationship of the parties. If they are husband and wife, it will probably be a joint tenancy or possibly even a tenancy by the entirety, if still recognized in the particular state. If the parties are unrelated and the document is silent as to type of tenancy, it will probably be a tenancy in common.

The tenancy by the entirety, a special form of joint ownership for husband and wife, is recognized in some states and not in others. Still others have modified versions of it, but where it does exist it is basically simimlar to a joint tenancy with survivorship rights.

Because of the many unique problems with the different types of co-tenancies and particularly with the joint tenancy, it seems generally preferable to use a living trust instead. Although a trust may be more complicated and expensive, any such complications and expense do not hold a candle to the potential complications and expense of a contested joint tenancy and the legal, tax, and emotional drain that go along with it. Nevertheless, many of us insist on continuing to run these risks for ourselves and our families, so the following is an effort to help you put it all together for that joint property you wish to transfer to a trust and that property you intend to keep in joint names.

1. BANK ACCOUNTS

THIS IS PERHAPS THE MOST popular subject of joint tenancy as well as the one that causes the most family grief. As discussed in Chapter 7, Joint Bank Accounts, the rights to this type of account on the death of a joint tenant can be quite fragile. Of course, if no one objects, the surviving joint tenant may withdraw the funds to his or her heart's content, regardless of the intent of the deceased. The trouble is that the attraction of the "found money" in the bank account itself attracts objections, and therefore a problem should be expected.

To avoid these objections and the costs associated with them, it is usually a better idea to hold the account in the form of a trust, *not* a trustee bank account, but a bank account in the name of *your* trust. Under this account a copy of your trust is left with the bank for its records so it may see who has authority to deal with the account. When this is done it is the *terms of your trust,* not the bank signature card, that will dictate the dispositions of this account during your life and after your death.

As previously discussed, you may be the trustee while you are able, so you will have complete control of your funds. If you should be unable to continue, a successor trustee, named by you, will take over. Unlike a joint tenant, the successor trustee must act according to the terms of your trust, and again, *unlike* a joint tenant, he cannot use the money for his own benefit, unless, of course, you have allowed him to do so under the trust.

Once your attorney has prepared your living trust and you have made the decision to fund it, you should take a *copy* of the signed trust to your bank and have the bank either change the title on the existing accounts or simply open up a *new* account in the name of your trust. The bank will usually want to keep a copy of your trust on file, but this is acceptable since its privacy is still respected.

If you are asked for a tax identification number, you should give the bank your social security number, since all interest on the account will be taxed to you. If the bank insists on a trust ID number, this is still not a problem, as discussed below in section 7.

Once you have opened a new account in the name of your trust, nothing else will change. You may make deposits and withdrawals, loans, open new accounts, and anything else you would do on your own. The difference is that now the funds in the account are "managed and disposed" according to the detailed terms of your trust rather than according to chance.

2. STOCKS AND BONDS

TRANSFERRING SECURITIES TO your trust can be a little more involved than with a bank account, but do not be discouraged. Whatever it takes, it's worth it.

If the securities are *registered* in joint names, you must first determine whether or not you want to transfer them to your trust. Remember that for income tax purposes the dividends or interest on these securities will be taxed to each joint owner equally. If this is saving you some income taxes, this might be a consideration. On the other hand, you will not save any estate taxes (the securities will be fully taxed in your estate, assuming you paid for them, unless the other joint tenant is your spouse; then only half will be included in your estate). Further, you may lose any right to leave them to someone else since they'll probably pass to the surviving joint tenant.

If, after proper estate and tax planning advice, it appears that they should not be left in joint names, you should consider transferring them to your living trust. One potential problem here is that if they are *registered* in joint names with another who did not contribute to the purchase price, there may be gift tax implications when the noncontributing tenant consents to transfer his share to your trust. To avoid this, you must establish that there never was a true joint tenancy, that no gift was ever intended, and that the other joint tenant was merely acting so as a matter of convenience, and so never had a real interest in the securities. Usually, this is established by testimony and the acts of the parties, unless you have a written (although informal) agreement between you, merely stating that one is acting for the other purely for his or her convenience and not as a true joint tenant. It may well be that you never have to offer this "proof" if the transfer is not questioned, and chances are, it will not be.

A transfer of registered securities to your living trust is effected by having each joint tenant sign the back of the stock certificate (or a "stock power," which is a separate paper, available from your stockbroker) and by submitting these to the transfer agent whose name will appear on the certificate. Before sending these, you must have the signatures "guaranteed" by a stockbrokerage house or by a bank, so the transfer agent can rely on their authenticity. (Certificates should always be sent by registered or certified mail.)

A much easier way of transferring securities is through your stockbroker. If the securities are in street name (held by your broker) or are registered, you may simply open a new brokerage account in the name of your trust and have your broker place the joint securities into this new account. If you intend to take delivery of the securities, you will ask him to re-register them in the name of the trust. Once transferred to the account or re-registered, they are considered to be in the trust and will be disposed according to its terms. (Your broker will undoubtedly ask for a copy of the trust.)

After the transfer, you, as trustee of your trust, may deal with the securities as if you personally owned them. There will be no restrictions, except that if you want to trade on margin or deal with options, the brokerage house (for its own protection) will usually request special language in your trust. If you intend to make these transactions, instruct your attorney when the trust is being drafted. If you forgot or did not know, you may amend the trust to add the necessary language (the brokerage house will be glad to tell you the specific language they would like).

As with the bank account, you may "wheel and deal" with your stocks without interference, and if you are disabled, your successor trustee may take over but his wheeling and dealing is subject to more scrutiny by yourself and your beneficiaries. You (and the successor trustee) must always remember that the successor trustee may be personally responsible if the terms of your trust are breached. In this way, you and your beneficiaries are protected.

3. REAL ESTATE

THIS TYPE OF PROPERTY IS unique in many respects. For one, every transaction with respect to the property is recorded at an official registry. The names of the old owners, the new owners, the mortgagees, discharge of mortgages, attachments, and so on are all on record. And where the real estate is transferred to a trust, the trust itself is recorded as well. Once the trust is recorded, it may be that any changes or amendments to your trust may also be required to be recorded, and in some cases this could be inconvenient. For this reason, attorneys have developed a simple form of trust especially designed to hold real estate.

This special trust, sometimes called a "nominee" trust, "realty" trust, or "blind" trust, discloses little more than the fact that the property is being held in trust by the named trustee (and a successor), that the beneficiaries are known to the trustee and that anyone dealing in good faith with the trustee may do so without worry of claim by the beneficiaries or others.

Because of its simplicity, amendments are needed infrequently, if ever, and so once recorded the trust may safely be used over and over for the real estate. The list or schedule of beneficiaries, however, must be coordinated with your living trust. As a matter of fact, the living trust is usually named as a beneficiary of the "blind" trust.

Once again, unless you are advised otherwise, the trusts are designed to give you complete and absolute control over all your property while you are alive (and able). The primary function of such trusts is to avoid probate court interference, and the attendant publicity, delays, and costs in the event of death or disability.

If your real estate is jointly owned with someone other than your spouse, you have the same potential gift tax problem on a transfer by the joint owners to your trust. In this case, you must (if questioned) establish the same basis as discussed above with jointly held securities—that is, that a gift was never intended. If the other joint tenant is your spouse, then the problem does not arise unless you previously elected to treat the tenancy as a gift and filed a gift tax return to that effect. Similarly a tenancy by the entirety in real estate may be transferred to the trust if both spouses consent.

Before you transfer any of your real estate to your trust, have your attorney advise you as to local law regarding the holding of real estate in a trust to be sure you are not creating any new problems. Further, if the property is mortgaged, be sure the transfer does not violate the terms of your mortgage. A bank holding a low-interest mortgage may like nothing better than to call the mortgage because of some technical breach of the mortgage, even though the new owners are essentially the same as the old. In some cases, you can simply prepare and sign the deeds without recording them. Your attorney can advise you.

4. BUSINESS INTERESTS

IT IS UNLIKELY THAT A business interest will be jointly held. If two or more persons own and run the business, chances are that it will be in the form of a partnership, and in that event each partner will own his share as the equivalent of a tenant in common. If the business is in the form of a corporation, however, it may be that the stock in the corporation is jointly held by the owner and someone else. If this is the case, we have the same considerations and potential problems that we would have with any jointly held property, except that in the case of a family business, it could be that this particular asset is much more valuable and important to the family than any other. If so, it becomes much more critical to handle it in a way that will minimize exposure to claims, court interference, and taxes. In my opinion, this is best done through a trust.

The trust to hold your business interests may be the very same living trust that holds your bank accounts and securities, or it may be a special, separate trust recommended by your attorney. Here, *particular* attention should be given to selection of the person or organization (the successor trustee) who will have control of the business after you. It should be someone capable of handling that responsibility. If the person or organization you wish to name as successor trustee is different from the person you wish to run your business, this can easily be arranged either by a separate trust or by a special provision in your primary trust. Remember that under a trust you can provide that control of the business will be in one person's name while benefits (payments of one type or another) may go to your family. If the business is jointly held, all of these choices are taken away from you.

5. OTHER PROPERTY

THERE IS VIRTUALLY NO TYPE of property that may not be transferred to a trust. Some property may lend itself to joint ownership because it is not important enough to bother transferring to a trust. It is often felt that tangible personal property falls into this category. Tangible personal property (TPP) is any property that can be "touched," except real estate and buildings on real estate. It also excludes stocks, bonds, and bank accounts—these are known as intangible personal property.

TPP, then, would commonly be furniture, clothing, jewelry, cars, clothes, coins, stamps, and so forth. More often than not such items have a sentimental value as well as an actual value and are seldom the subject of a joint tenancy. In some states, however, there is a presumption that husband and wife hold the TPP in their residence as joint tenants with rights of survivorship. This enables the surviving spouse to continue to use all such property without interference. If the property is not exceptionally valuable, it is all right to let this presumption stand. If the parties are not husband and wife, it is a good idea to make a written declaration that the property is in the joint names of the applicable parties, with rights of survivorship.

If the property is of considerable value—obviously this could be $5,000 in some estates, $50,000 in others—then some specific attention should be given to its disposition. Surprisingly, it is the tangible property—the clock, the diamond ring, the piano, the oriental rug, the silver, and grandma's set of china—that often are the center of the bitterest fights and will contests. You should think about the desired disposition, then attach a statement to your trust declaring that such items are being held in trust and that they should be divided in a certain way on your death. This way you will avoid the expenses of probate and probably avoid the bitter fights as well.

For example, the following statement might be prepared, signed, and kept with your trust: "I hereby transfer the following items to the John Johnston trust dated 8/19/81 and declare that I hold said items in trust to be held and distributed in accordance with the terms thereof [list the items, carefully describing each one], signed John Johnston donor and trustee, 12/23/81."

In addition, you could amend your trust by adding a provision disposing of the TPP after your death. Perhaps something like this: "I hereby amend the John Johnston Trust dated 8/19/81 by adding the following paragraph: 'The items of tangible personal property contributed to this trust on 12/23/81 and listed on the transfer of the same date shall be distributed as follows on the Donor's death: [list the particular items and the names of those persons who are to receive them]. If any of the aforesaid persons should predecease me then the item or items which would have passed to him or her shall then pass to———' [or 'according to the remaining terms of the trust']."

6. PROPERTY HELD AS A TENANT IN COMMON

IF THE CO-TENANCY IN question is a tenancy in common rather than a joint tenancy or a tenancy by the entirety, then a transfer to your trust is perhaps even more imperative if avoiding probate is one of your objectives; otherwise your common interest in the property will pass through your estate and not to the surviving tenant. To transfer your undivided interest in the tenancy in common to your trust, you may follow the general instructions above for the various types of property. After the transfer to your trust is completed, you as trustee of your trust, and not as an individual, will be a tenant in common with the other co-tenant or tenants.

7. OPERATION OF YOUR TRUST
—NOT TO WORRY

THE CONCEPT OF HAVING MOST or all of your property in a trust may tend to scare you a little, but once it is done and understood, you will quickly get used to it and discover it is no more difficult than belonging to the Book-of-the-Month Club.

The first scare often occurs when you discover that you must transfer your property to your trust to make the whole thing work. Changing bank accounts, securities, business interests, and real estate can cause you to have second thoughts about the trust and question whether you're "doing the right thing." If this happens, remember that your trust is revocable—you can change it or cancel it, in whole or in part, anytime you wish at your absolute whim. So even if you later felt that you weren't "doing the right thing," you need only to reverse the process and take all your property back.

The second scare sometimes occurs if you apply for a tax identification number for your trust from the IRS. You are only required to do this if neither you nor your spouse is a trustee of your revocable trust. If *you* are the trustee of your own trust, or if *your spouse* is the trustee, or if either you or your spouse is a co-trustee with someone else, you *do not* need to apply for a separate trust identification number, as long as you file a joint income tax return with your spouse. You simply use *your own social security number* on all trust accounts, and report all dividends, interest, capital gains, or any other trust income (or losses) on your regular 1040 return as you normally would. The only time you'll apply for a separate trust identification number is when neither you nor your spouse is a trustee of your trust. In this case the IRS requires a trust tax return, and such a return calls for a tax identification number.

Most of us like to have as little to do with the IRS as possible, and notice from the IRS—any notice—is something we can do without. The fact is that once you apply for an ID number, the IRS assumes you (or rather the trust) will be filing an income tax return. If you don't file one for the trust or tell them why one isn't filed, they get concerned and may send you a notice. Don't panic! It does not mean you are under investigation or have any problem. It merely means they would like some information about the trust income.

Your revocable trust is called a "grantor" trust and as such, all the interest, dividends, and other incomes are taxed to you. To satisfy the IRS you need only file a "blank" form 1041 trust return with the name and address of the trust (your address), the total income, and include in an attached, *simple* statement that it is a grantor trust and all the income is reported by you the grantor. Such a statement might read as follows:

> IRS Form 1041— Schedule for Grantor Trust—The Grover W. Lambeck Trust
> GRANTOR: Grover W. Lambeck, ss no. 000-11-2222
> 11 Beacon Street, Boston, MA 02108
> *INCOME: Dividends $1,250
> Interest $2,100
> †DEDUCTIONS: NONE

*This is any income that is realized in the name of the trust. It does not have to be itemized. It is reported and itemized on the grantor's (Lambeck's) individual income tax return.

†These would be any deductions that "pass through" the trust, such as where the trust sells securities at a loss, where the trust borrows money and pays interest on the loan, where a tax shelter is held in the name of the trust, or where the trust holds income-producing real estate, which could show a loss.

If neither you nor your spouse is a trustee of your trust, a statement similar to the one above should be submitted each year with your "blank" 1041 trust return, and you should have no problem with the IRS (at least for this!), since the full details are shown on your individual return and the IRS is not getting "cheated." Remember, if you or your spouse is a trustee, you need not file anything except your individual return.

The same concept often applies to those states which have an income tax and which allow trust income to be "passed through" to the beneficiaries. Check with your accountant or tax lawyer to be sure of the treatment in your state.

Once you have separate trust accounts you will find it much easier to deal with banks and transfer agents through your trust. Further, you will become a little more accustomed to dealing with the trust yourself. In this respect, you will be buying and selling securities, opening accounts, etc. in the name of "John Smith, Trustee of the John Smith Trust, dated 12/1/82," instead of "John Smith," or "John and Mary Smith as joint tenants."

Remember, such freedom of movement and control is primarily because your trust is revocable. If you create an irrevocable trust, the rules are quite different and usually you will lose control of the property in the trust.

8. COORDINATING TRANSFERS TO YOUR TRUSTS

ALTHOUGH THE SEVERAL types of joint property may all be transferred to a single trust, it may be that on the recommendations of your attorney and other advisors, more than one trust is necessary. If this is so, you should be sure that the terms and provisions of each trust are coordinated with one another and with your overall plan. Lack of proper coordination among several trusts can create more problems and exposure than they avoid. This is the classic problem of the popular "blank forms" books.

Once your plan and trusts are completed, consider having the whole package reviewed once again by another expert—a second opinion—to be sure the entire plan is properly coordinated to accomplish your objectives with a minimum of delays and expense. The cost of a second opinion is usually nominal since it involves only a review of what has already been done.

If your plan calls for only one trust and all your property has been transferred to it, you should nevertheless make a checklist of what is in it and keep the list up to date. New property should, if this is your plan, be acquired in the name of your trust rather than individually, and the whole arrangement ought to be reviewed once each year.

9. WHAT YOU MIGHT LEAVE IN JOINT NAMES

IDEALLY, MY ANSWER TO THIS IS nothing. The problems relating to joint ownership apply to the very concept of joint ownership—the type or amount of property is largely incidental. If this is so, then no property should be held in joint names. There are, however, practical considerations and limitations to any theoretical approach. For one thing, many of the problems referred to are the result of some unforeseen incident, some accident, incompetence or disability, conflicting claim, disgruntled heir, or other contingency. If there are no such claims, no disability, no disgruntled heirs, no simultaneous death, or no objections, then the joint property may pass trouble-free!

This is not so far-fetched. In many families, jointly held property passes freely from one member to another and except for the additional estate taxes (often a major factor) it poses no problem because there are no objections or other obstacles. It is, however, a risk, and the more property involved, the greater the risk and the more foolhardy is the person who takes it. Therefore, the ideas and recommendations discussed above should be considered for most if not all of your joint property.

There may be, however, a need or desire to leave something in joint names, and in fact, it is acceptable in moderation, provided you realize the risks involved. A small bank account, for example, between husband and wife may offer a surviving spouse easy access to funds in the event of death or disability (but so would a trust!). The amount that may be considered small would vary from family to family, but something like $6,000 to $10,000 would seem appropriate. Similarly, the principal residence is often left in joint names between the spouses, since it seems that this arrangement is seldom the object of an attack. However, these two observations should in no way be taken as recommendations. They are more an acknowledgment of use and custom, and, if they are continued, should be done so only with an understanding of the risks of such things as simultaneous death, remarriage of a spouse, estate taxes, and probate of the property on the death of the survivor.

If for some reason you decide to continue any or all of your property in joint ownership form with your spouse and/or children and/or others, think back on all the cases and related problems discussed in this book and reconsider. If you still persist and cannot kick the joint property habit, then at least do these two things:

A. Get into the habit of "documenting" your intent with respect to the joint property. Tax questions aside, if you want your son or daughter, or niece, nephew, or even secretary to have the proceeds (or *not* to have the proceeds) of a bank account or other items of property held in joint names with them, then say so in writing. A diary, letter, or informal statement relating to the particular account and the particular joint tenant clearly indicating your intent might be just the evidence needed to avoid a protracted and expensive contest.

But try not to get carried away with your statement. Remember it is not intended to be a will or a trust—just a statement of your intent confirming (or denying) the survivorship interest. Many convenience accounts invite problems because no evidence is available to show the deceased's intent. If you open an account with a friend purely as a convenience to you so she can manage your funds, be sure to let the right people—family, lawyer, other close friends—know this in writing. Otherwise, the family could lose funds or property that you wanted them to have.

The statement or letter may be quite informal: "Dear Bill, this is to let you know that I have opened two joint bank acounts with my friend Helen Oates. One is at the First National Bank of Wichita and the other is at the Wichita Trust Company. Since I have been ill and unable to get to the bank I need someone who will help me pay bills, reinvest the funds, etc., and Helen has agreed to do this. She realizes that should anything happen to me, the money belongs to you and your sister, equally, as I have provided in my will. Love, Mother. 3/21/81."

(Although this statement would no doubt prevent Helen from taking the funds as surviving joint tenant, it would likewise throw the funds into Mother's probate estate so as to pass under the terms of her will. This result could be avoided, with the convenience arrangement retained, by holding the funds in a trust, with Helen as trustee instead of joint tenant.)

Another statement with a different intent might read: "Dear Bill, this is in reference to the joint bank account I opened with you at the California National Bank. Should anything happen to me I want these funds to be yours if you survive me. Even though the rest of my estate passes to you and your sister equally, these funds should pass to you in addition to what you receive under my will. Love, Mother. 3/21/81."

If Bill survives his mother, he should receive the funds. If he predeceases her, the money will pass through her probate estate. In either event, mother's intent of division of her estate is clear, even though the will and the joint accounts are inconsistent with one another, and this illustrates the second habit to develop.

B. Review the joint accounts periodically to see if they *still* reflect your wishes and look at them in the light of your will and/or trust to see if there are conflicting provisions. If so, clarify your intent in writing and consider adding a provision to your will and trust as follows (or something similar as may be recommended by your attorney):

> Declaration of Intent. This is to acknowledge that I have deposited funds in certain savings accounts* in the joint names of myself and my son, Bill. In the event my said son survives me, it is my considered purpose and intent that the contents of any such accounts shall, upon my death, become his sole and absolute property as surviving joint tenant, by operation of law, and that the funds therein are not to be considered a part of my probate estate, nor are they to be considered as being disposed of by this will.

Keep in mind that the above provision and the recommended letter and statements are not foolproof. They can be quite effective to indicate your intent, and most cases of joint account contests turn on proof of intent of the deceased joint tenant (unless the deceased contributed nothing to the property). In any event, it cannot hurt to clarify the picture.

In spite of all the warnings, obvious problems, and potential expense connected with joint ownership, it is certain that it will continue to be one of the more popular ways to hold property. However, if this book has convinced you to place even a portion of your property in trust and to prepare even a few letters or statements reflecting your intent for your joint property, then you will have avoided some of the problems and expenses, and an important purpose will have been served.

---

*This could be reworded to cover any other type of property.

GLOSSARY

ADMINISTRATION EXPENSES	All the expenses connected with settling an estate including executor's or administrator's fees, attorney's and accountant's fees, court fees, and the expenses related to estate property.
ADMINISTRATOR	A person named by a court to handle the settlement of the estate of a person who dies without a will, or for a deceased who had a will but no named executor.
BASIS	The cost of an item of property to determine gain or loss for income tax purposes.
BEARER BONDS	Bonds (such as municipal or treasury bonds) that are payable to the bearer—the person in possession, rather than any named individual.

209

BENEFICIARY

A person who is entitled to receive benefits (usually money or other property) from a trust or an estate.

COMMON PROPERTY

Property that is held by two or more parties under one of the forms of co-ownership, i.e., joint tenancy, tenancy in common, tenancy by the entirety, or community property.

CONVENIENCE ACCOUNT

An account—usually a bank account—that has been opened in joint names but only for the convenience of one of the joint owners and *not* with the intent that the noncontributing owner receive the balance in the account.

CORPORATE TRUSTEE

A professional organization such as a bank or a trust company that receives, holds, and manages money and other property from members of the public under a trust agreement.

CO-TENANCY

When two or more parties own the same property at the same time and the property remains undivided.

CO-TENANT

One of the owners under a cotenancy.

CO-TRUSTEE

Another person, often a family member, who serves with the trustee in helping to make decisions concerning the trust.

COST BASIS

Same as "Basis."

DONEE

A person who receives a gift.

DONOR

A person who makes a gift; sometimes one who creates a trust (see "Settlor").

EQUITY

(In a property sense) The net value of an interest in property after all charges or encumbrances (e.g., mortgage) are subtracted.

EXECUTOR

A person (or organization) named in a will to handle the settlement of

FAMILY TRUST

the estate according to the will. In common usage, a trust agreement that provides for a certain portion of the estate or trust to be set aside in a separate trust to operate for the benefit of the family (spouse or children or both).

FIDUCIARY

Anyone responsible for the custody or management of property belonging to others such as an executor, administrator, or trustee.

FIDUCIARY DUTY

The high degree of trust, responsibility, and objectiveness required of anyone acting as a fiduciary.

FUNDING

The transfer of property to a trust.

GIFT

The transfer of property from one individual to another without consideration.

GIFT TAX

The federal (and sometimes state) tax levied on the act of making a gift, usually charged to the donor.

GIFT TAX EXCLUSION

The amount of a gift that is not subject to a gift tax, usually measured or allowed on an annual basis.

GRANTOR

A person who creates a trust—also called Donor, Settlor, Creator.

GRANTOR TRUST

A trust that, for income tax purposes, is treated as owned by the grantor and that therefore results in all income of the trust being taxed to him.

INTANGIBLE PERSONAL PROPERTY

Property other than real estate and other than property which can be "touched." Examples of intangible property: stocks, bonds, bank accounts, copyrights, patents, etc., as they all merely represent the right to receive something of value.

INTER-VIVOS TRUST

A trust created while the creator of it is alive—a "living" trust.

Irrevocable Trust — A trust that cannot be changed or revoked by the person who created it.

Joint Ownership — When two or more people own the same property at the same time in equal shares, with the understanding that on the death of any one, the survivor(s) will own the whole.

Joint Property — *Any* property in joint ownership form (*not* just real estate).

Joint-tenancy — Same as joint ownership.

Joint-tenant — One of the joint owners in a joint ownership or a joint tenancy.

Living Trust — A trust created during the creator's lifetime.

Marital Deduction — A deduction for estate and gift tax purposes for the amount of property that passes to a spouse.

Marital Deduction Trust — A trust established to receive an amount on behalf of the surviving spouse which qualifies for the marital deduction.

Married Women's Act — Generally, laws passed in most states that give a married woman legal individuality—i.e., the right to deal as if she were a single person.

Partition — The right of a co-tenant to have the commonly held property divided by court order.

Personal Property — Any property other than real estate.

Probate — The procedure in each state required to legally settle the estate of a deceased person and transfer his "probate property."

Probate Property — Property that may be transferred only through the probate procedure, and that would therefore include property or proceeds payable to the estate of the deceased.

Real Estate — Land and permanent buildings on the land.

REAL PROPERTY	Same as real estate.
REGISTERED SECURITIES	Stocks or bonds that state on the certificate the name or names of the owners according to company records.
REVOCABLE TRUST	A trust that may at any time be altered, amended, or revoked by the creator.
RIGHT OF SEVERANCE	The right of a co-tenant to separate or divide commonly held property under a joint tenancy or a tenancy in common.
RIGHT OF SURVIVORSHIP	The right of a joint tenant (but *not* a tenant in common) to take the whole of the jointly held property if he survives the other joint tenant(s).
SETTLOR	A person who creates a trust.
SEVERANCE	The act of dividing commonly held property.
SPENDTHRIFT PROVISION	The provision in a trust agreement that allows the donor to place the share of the beneficiary out of reach of the beneficiary's creditors. The funds of this particular beneficiary (other than the donor) while in the trust cannot be attached or recovered by someone suing the beneficiary.
STEPPED-UP COST BASIS	An increased (usually) tax cost that takes effect when property is received as the result of a person's death.
STREET-NAME SECURITIES	Stocks or bonds of a customer that are held in the name of the brokerage house for ease of transfer.
SUCCESSOR EXECUTOR	A person named in a will to replace the first-named executor if for any reason he is not able to serve.
SUCCESSOR TRUSTEE	A person appointed to replace the original trustee when the original trustee ceases to serve as trustee for any reason.

TANGIBLE PERSONAL PROPERTY

Property other than real estate that can be touched, such as jewelry, furniture, clothing, automobiles, boats, machinery, etc.

TENANCY BY THE ENTIRETY

A special form of joint tenancy in which only husband and wife can be co-tenants and neither (alone) can cause a division of the property.

TENANCY IN COMMON

When two or more parties own the same property at the same time, but not necessarily in equal shares, and there is no right of survivorship, so that a deceased co-tenant's share passes through his estate.

TRANSFEREE

One who receives transferred property.

TRANSFEROR

One who transfers property.

TRUST

A relationship in which one person (the trustee) is the holder of the legal title to property (the trust property) to keep or use for the benefit of another person (the beneficiary).

TRUSTEE

An individual or professional organization who holds the legal title to property for the benefit of another person or persons.

UNDIVIDED INTEREST

A share of property that has not been physically set aside or divided, such as a joint interest in a home.

UNIFIED CREDIT

A tax credit, allowed by the federal government, which may be applied toward either gift or estate taxes that may be due.

NOTES

CHAPTER 4

Page 36   [1]States that still recognize some form of tenancy by the entirety: Alaska, Arkansas, Delaware, Florida, Hawaii, Indiana, Kentucky, Maryland, Massachusetts, Michigan, Mississippi, Missouri, New Jersey, New York, North Carolina, Oregon, Pennsylvania, Rhode Island, Tennessee, Vermont, Virgin Islands, Virginia, Wyoming, and the District of Columbia.

Page 37   [2]Community property states: Arizona, California, Idaho, Louisiana, Nevada, New Mexico, Texas, and Washington.

CHAPTER 8

Page 116   [1]The following states *do not allow access* (or allow only *limited access*) to a box on the death of a renter unless a state tax agent has examined the contents: Arizona, California, Colorado, Idaho, Illinois, Indiana, Iowa, Kentucky, Louisiana,

Michigan, Minnesota, Missouri, New Hampshire, New Jersey, New York, North Carolina, North Dakota, Ohio, Oklahoma, Oregon, Pennsylvania, South Carolina, South Dakota, Tennessee, Texas, Utah, Washington, Wisconsin, Wyoming, and the District of Columbia.

The following states *allow unrestricted access* to a jointly rented box on the death of a joint owner: Alabama, Alaska, Arkansas, Connecticut, Delaware, Florida, Georgia, Hawaii, Kansas, Maine, Maryland, Massachusetts, Mississippi, Montana, Nebraska, Nevada, New Mexico, Rhode Island, Vermont, Virginia, West Virginia.

The above information is reasonably current, but you should make a check of the laws in your state to determine whether changes have been recently made.

The following list will help you find the applicable safe deposit laws in your state.

(1) ALABAMA		Ala. Code vol. 22, § 43-1-40
(2) ALASKA		Alaska Stat. § 13.11.320
(3) ARIZONA	a.	Ariz. Rev. Stat. §§ 6-921 to 29
	b.	Ariz. Rev. Stat. §§ 6-235 to 36
	c.	Ariz. Rev. Stat. § 42-1530
(4) ARKANSAS		Ark. Stat. Ann. § 62-2103
(5) CALIFORNIA		Cal. Rev. & Tax Code §§ 1432-48
(6) COLORADO	a.	Colo. Rev. Stat. § 39-23.5
	b.	Colo. Rev. Stat. § 11-9-101 to 106
	c.	Colo. Rev. Stat. § 15-10-111
(7) CONNECTICUT	a.	Conn. Gen Stat. Ann. § 45-164
	b.	Conn. Gen Stat. Ann § 45-164 (a)
(8) DELAWARE		Del. Code tit. 12, § 1301
(9) FLORIDA		Fla. Stat. Ann. §§ 659.48 to .51
(10) GEORGIA	a.	Ga. Code Ann. § 41A-1609
	b.	Ga. Code Ann. § 113-610
(11) HAWAII		Haw. Rev. Stat. § 531-20
(12) IDAHO	a.	Idaho Code § 14-417
	b.	Idaho Code § 15-2-902
(13) ILLINOIS	a.	Ill. Ann. Stat. ch. 114, § 359
	b.	Ill. Ann. Stat. ch. 3, § 60
(14) INDIANA	a.	Ind. Code § 6-4.1-8-5 to 8
	b.	Ind. Code § 29-1-7-3
(15) IOWA	a.	Iowa Code Ann. § 524.810
	b.	Iowa Code Ann. § 524-809
	c.	Iowa Code Ann. § 450.86
(16) KANSAS		Kan. Stat. § 9-1301 to 7

(17) KENTUCKY	a.	Ky. Rev. Stat. § 394.160
	b.	Ky. Rev. Stat. § 140.250
	c.	Ky. Rev. Stat. § 132.420
(18) LOUISIANA	a.	La. Civ. Code Ann. art. 6, § 66.1
	b.	La. Rev. Stat. Ann. § 47:2413
(19) MAINE		Me. Rev. Stat. tit. 18, § 9
(20) MARYLAND	a.	Md. Ann. Code art. 4, § 202
	b.	Md. Ann. Code art. 23, § 315-16
(21) MASSACHUSETTS		Mass. Ann. Laws ch. 191, § 13
(22) MICHIGAN	a.	Mich. Comp. Laws Ann. § 707.7
	b.	Mich. Comp. Laws Ann. § 205.209
(23) MINNESOTA	a.	Minn. Stat. Ann. § 291.20
	b.	Minn. Stat. Ann § 55.10
	c.	Minn. Stat. Ann. § 525.221
(24) MISSISSIPPI		Miss. Code Ann. § 91-7-5
(25) MISSOURI	a.	Mo. Ann. Stat. § 145.210
	b.	Mo. Ann. Stat. § 473.043
(26) MONTANA	a.	Mont. Rev. Codes Ann. § 91A-2-902
	b.	Mont. Rev. Codes Ann. § 67-309
(27) NEBRASKA	a.	Neb. Rev. Stat. § 30-2355 to 6
(28) NEVADA		Nev. Rev. Stat. § 136.050
(29) NEW HAMPSHIRE	a.	N.H. Rev. Stat. Ann. § 552:2
	b.	N.H. Rev. Stat. Ann. §§ 86:72 to 76
(30) NEW JERSEY	a.	N.J. Stat. Ann. § 54:35-19
	b.	N.J. Stat. Ann. § 3A:3-23
	c.	N.J. Stat. Ann § 46:39-4
(31) NEW MEXICO	a.	N.M. Stat. Ann. § 58-1-11
	b.	N.M. Stat. Ann. § 58-1-14
	c.	N.M. Stat. Ann. § 58-10-108
(32) NEW YORK	a.	N.Y. Sur. Ct. Pro. Law § 2003
	b.	N.Y. Tax Law art. 10, § 227
	c.	N.Y. Tax Law art. 10C, § 249cc
	d.	N.Y. Tax Law art. 10, § 228
	e.	N.Y. Tax Law art. 10C, § 249 to 249mm
(33) NORTH CAROLINA	a.	N.C. Gen. Stat. § 105-24
	b.	N.C. Gen Stat. § 31-15
(34) NORTH DAKOTA	a.	N.D. Cent. Code § 30.1-11-01 to 02
	b.	N.D. Cent. Code § 57-37.1-12 to 13
(35) OHIO	a.	Ohio Rev. Code Ann. § 2107.09
	b.	Ohio Rev. Code Ann. § 5731.39

(36) OKLAHOMA	a.	Okla. Stat. Ann. tit. 6, § 1308
	b.	Okla. Stat. Ann. tit. 68, § 812
(37) OREGON	a.	Ore. Rev. Stat. § 118.440
	b.	Ore. Rev. Stat. § 112.425
(38) PENNSYLVANIA	a.	Pa. Stat. Ann. tit. 7, § 609
	b.	Pa. Stat. Ann. tit. 72, § 2485-1101 to 1153
(39) RHODE ISLAND		R.I. Gen. Laws § 33-7-5
(40) SOUTH CAROLINA	a.	S.C. Code § 34-19-50
	b.	S.C. Code §12-15-560
(41) SOUTH DAKOTA	a.	S.D. Compiled Laws Ann. § 30-6-1
	b.	S.D. Compiled Laws Ann. §§ 10-41-47 to 48
	c.	S.D. Compiled Laws Ann. §§ 51-23-1 to 10
(42) TENNESSEE	a.	Tenn. Code Ann. § 45-419
	b.	Tenn. Code Ann. § 30-1632
(43) TEXAS	a.	Tex. Tax-Gen. Ann. art. 14.21
	b.	Tex. Tax-Gen. Ann. art. 14.22
(44) UTAH	a.	Utah Code Ann. § 59-12-34
	b.	Utah Code Ann. § 75-2-902
(45) VERMONT		Vt. Stat. Ann. tit. 14, § 103
(46) VIRGINIA		Va. Code §§ 6.1-331 to 42
(47) WASHINGTON	a.	Wash. Rev. Code Ann. § 83.44.030
	b.	Wash. Rev. Code Ann. § 11.20.030
(48) WEST VIRGINIA		W. Va. Code § 41-5-1
(49) WISCONSIN	a.	Wis. Stat. Ann § 856.05
	b.	Wis. Stat. Ann. § 72.11
(50) WYOMING		Wyo. Stat. § 2-4-201
(51) DISTRICT OF COLUMBIA	a.	D.C. Code § 26-202
	b.	D.C. Code § 47-1624

INDEX

ABOUT THE AUTHOR

Alexander A. Bove, Jr., is senior partner of the Boston law firm of Bove, Charmoy & McDougald, which concentrates its practice in the areas of estate and business planning and tax law. He has authored numerous articles on trusts, wills, probate, family financial planning and estate planning, as well as two books on estate taxes; and his well-known "Family Money" column has appeared weekly in *The Boston Globe* since 1973.

Mr. Bove has lectured extensively to public as well as professional groups and is currently on the faculty of Northeastern University Law School, where he teaches estate planning. After obtaining his Juris Doctor degree, Mr. Bove earned the advanced degree of Master of Laws in Taxation. In addition to his many years in the practice of law, his background and experience encompass the fields of investments, insurance and financial planning.